THE ART OF COCKTAILS

BY THE LEGENDARY
BARTENDER AT THE RITZ

FRANK MEIER

EDITED BY **PHILIPPE COLLIN**

ILLUSTRATIONS BY **DELIUS**

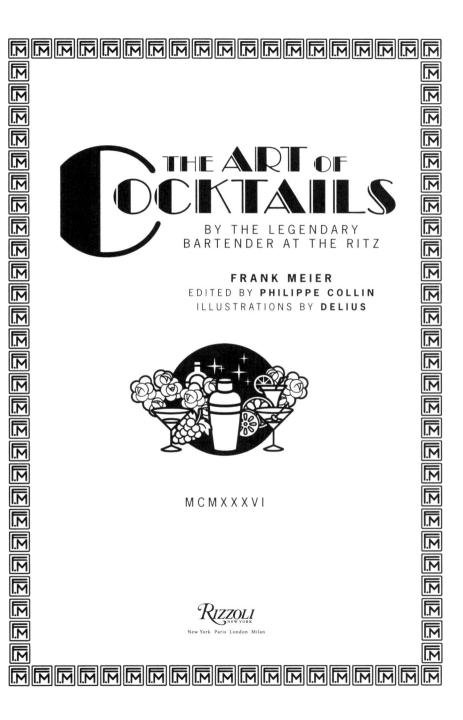

MCMXXXVI

RIZZOLI
NEW YORK

New York Paris London Milan

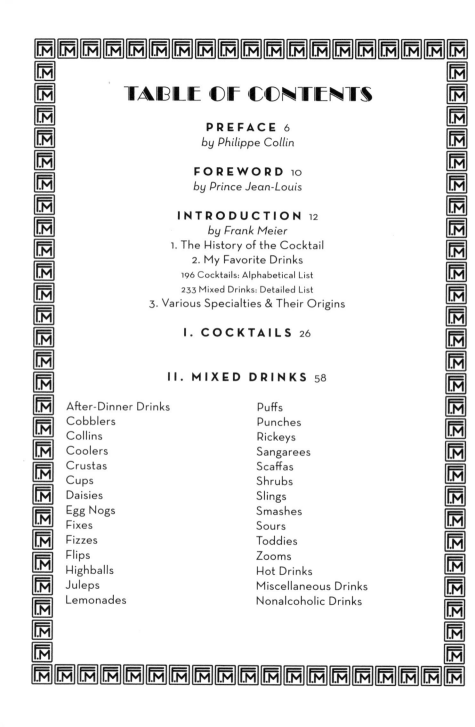

TABLE OF CONTENTS

PREFACE 6
by Philippe Collin

FOREWORD 10
by Prince Jean-Louis

INTRODUCTION 12
by Frank Meier
1. The History of the Cocktail
2. My Favorite Drinks
196 Cocktails: Alphabetical List
233 Mixed Drinks: Detailed List
3. Various Specialties & Their Origins

I. COCKTAILS 26

II. MIXED DRINKS 58

After-Dinner Drinks
Cobblers
Collins
Coolers
Crustas
Cups
Daisies
Egg Nogs
Fixes
Fizzes
Flips
Highballs
Juleps
Lemonades

Puffs
Punches
Rickeys
Sangarees
Scaffas
Shrubs
Slings
Smashes
Sours
Toddies
Zooms
Hot Drinks
Miscellaneous Drinks
Nonalcoholic Drinks

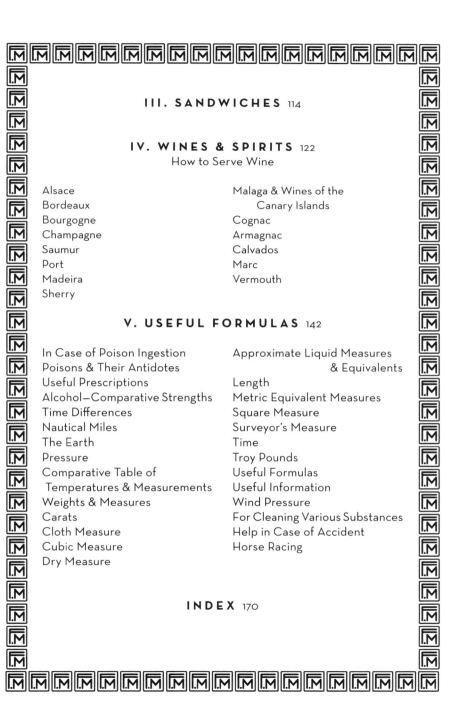

III. SANDWICHES 114

IV. WINES & SPIRITS 122
How to Serve Wine

Alsace
Bordeaux
Bourgogne
Champagne
Saumur
Port
Madeira
Sherry

Malaga & Wines of the
  Canary Islands
Cognac
Armagnac
Calvados
Marc
Vermouth

V. USEFUL FORMULAS 142

In Case of Poison Ingestion
Poisons & Their Antidotes
Useful Prescriptions
Alcohol—Comparative Strengths
Time Differences
Nautical Miles
The Earth
Pressure
Comparative Table of
  Temperatures & Measurements
Weights & Measures
Carats
Cloth Measure
Cubic Measure
Dry Measure

Approximate Liquid Measures
  & Equivalents
Length
Metric Equivalent Measures
Square Measure
Surveyor's Measure
Time
Troy Pounds
Useful Formulas
Useful Information
Wind Pressure
For Cleaning Various Substances
Help in Case of Accident
Horse Racing

INDEX 170

PREFACE

Move aside, amateur cocktail enthusiasts! *The Art of Cocktails* is much more than a book of drink recipes. This unclassifiable guide you hold in your hands is a reissue of a fashionable accessory, first published in 1936. Coveted and sought after by the high society of the time, this rare item was printed in only a thousand copies and exclusively in English for a carefully selected international clientele. Here, you will find beverages that are both surprisingly simple and sophisticated. More importantly, you will uncover the world of a bygone era, that of the aesthetes of the interwar period.

The author, Frank Meier, has been forgotten. Yet he was the most illustrious of bartenders, even enjoying a worldwide reputation in elite circles. Born in Austria in 1884, he became a French citizen in 1921 after serving in the Foreign Legion during World War I. Meier was celebrated for his cocktail art by the most elegant drinkers in Europe and North America. His fine mustache, precise gestures, and twinkling eye were as famous as his subtle dosages. Frank Meier, a child of the Austrian proletariat, moved to London and then New York at the beginning of the twentieth century, where Charles Mahoney, the cocktail master of the prestigious Hoffman House hotel, taught him the art of mixing drinks. This social elevator took Frank Meier to the Place Vendôme in Paris. At the Ritz, he befriended Cole Porter, Ernest Hemingway, F. Scott Fitzgerald, Florence Jay Gould, Jean Cocteau, Sacha Guitry, and Kermit Roosevelt, son of U.S. president Theodore Roosevelt. In fifteen years, Meier became an essential figure among the elite. From his bar, he created a haven for the upper bourgeoisie. He was feared, for his hospitality was selective: only the crème de la crème. In the mid-1930s, no other bar in the world had such a distinguished clientele. It was

the fief of the overlords of the
night, Parisian poets, New York
writers, and wealthy, lighthearted
heirs. This was his life's work:
the marriage of aristocracy and
bohemia. From the dawn of the
Roaring Twenties, Meier was a
confidant, and often a counselor,
to the powerful clients of the Ritz
until the eve of World War II.

It is them—and only them—that Meier had in mind when he wrote *The Artistry of Mixing Drinks*. Thus, this book aimed to be a complete, precise, and refined memento for the most eminent personalities of the 1930s. Owning a copy meant you belonged to a very exclusive club.

Immersing yourself in *The Art of Cocktails* is an astonishing journey through time in which you will discover all sorts of things. First, of course, the cocktail recipes. Over four hundred of them, many of which were created by the master himself. To recognize them, look for the initials "FM" in Art Deco style. Each of these beverages, with poetic or mysterious names, holds a story. When recreating Meier's subtle mixes today, one is immediately struck by how few ingredients used: three, sometimes four, rarely more. Through his cocktail recipes, one can discern his taste for sophisticated sobriety, the definition of elegance in the eyes of this upstart who became the darling of the wealthy. For Meier, simplicity was the golden rule of luxury. *The Artistry of Mixing Drinks* was also, and above all, an extraordinary *vade mecum* for the rich drinkers of the early twentieth century. Thus, one also encounters a plethora of curious advice and strange information, such as first aid instructions in case of drowning, sunstroke, or snake bites, formulas for physics and geometry, or the proper way to serve wines. Add to this some sandwich recipes, conversion and measurement tables, wind pressure maps, including surprising things like advice on how to sharpen dull files or a brief history of horse racing, Meier's passion.

Such was the high society of the interwar period—a universe of refined diplomats and cosmopolitan dandies who, undoubtedly blinded by the luxury of the Ritz, did not sense what was brewing around them throughout Europe. They clinked their glasses, unaware their world was crumbling, before being ruined and corrupted in the trials of World War II. In its own way, though somewhat frivolous, this precious book reveals a past shrouded in a veil that is interesting to lift now, so many years later. I must thank

Nicolas de Cointet, a talented publisher, without whom *The Art of Cocktails* would not have this second life. Here is a formidable *mise en abyme* considering the uncommon fate of Meier during the Nazi occupation of Paris between 1940 and 1944. But that is another story to be discovered in my book, *The Bartender of the Ritz*.*

PHILIPPE COLLIN
Historian, writer, and producer of history podcasts

*Originally published in French as *Le Barman du Ritz* by Philippe Collin (Paris: Éditions Albin Michel, 2024).

FOREWORD

Though Frank Meier's primary object is to expound the art of mixing drinks, which he has studied and practiced so long, I feel that some mention should be made in this book regarding the institution of the American bar and the rare qualities the man behind it should possess.

What Europeans call an "American bar" is in fact international in its true sense. Visitors from all countries expect, and can have, their own special drinks; and while cocktails are perhaps the main raison d'être, this institution has various other points. It is, in a way, a meeting place where acquaintanceship and introductions are easy, and where, in consequence, the barriers of many inhibitions and shyness disappear without great formality. This definition is not intended to accuse American bars of democracy, or to deny the merits of "pubs," "bistros," or *Weinstuben*. Many readers undoubtedly have their pet pub or beer garden to back against any bar.

Few people realize that the mood of the man when having his drink is of the greatest importance: if the drink, the atmosphere of the place, and the bartender's smile and amiability are conducive to putting its patron in the right frame of mind, the success of such a place is certain.

The successful bartender must be a chemist, a physiologist, and a psychologist of the first order; in other words, the true mixologist is a man of science. Furthermore, he requires a deep understanding of humanity, an ability to sympathize with his patrons' real or fancied troubles, and laugh when they repeat a story that he had told them the day before. He must be able and willing to advise on almost any subject, from the proper diet for dogs or goldfish to selection of a restaurant or theater that would please their aunts or their business associates. He must see that they are served promptly and with good drinks and remember their individual preferences. He must develop some of the qualities of the chameleon yet retain a personality of his own. Tact is essential, as misunderstandings have a way of arising after the umpteenth drink. A good bartender really requires everything a diplomat should have and something more: an instinctive knowledge of gastronomy as well as wines and spirits.

Meier's book* enables anyone, whether at home or elsewhere, to enjoy the various drinks that he has made and served to a worldwide clientele. His many friends and admirers will welcome this work, which reveals the secret formulas. Even in his absence, they will be able to once more have those delicious drinks that Meier alone knows how to make. One element however will be lacking: the personality of the author and his mastery.

Jeanlouis
Prince de Viggiano

*This book is a new edition of the legendary guide published in 1936, newly illustrated for the occasion and presented by Philippe Collin, author of the novel *Le Barman du Ritz*, released in French (Paris: Éditions Albin Michel, 2024).

INTRODUCTION

1. THE HISTORY OF THE COCKTAIL

Many will ask what is the origin of cocktails. In compiling this book on the art of mixing drinks, I have recently had the occasion to investigate the origin of the name "cocktails." The inventor of this boon to mankind will perhaps always remain unknown. But in going through some old documents, I find the following story, which, authentic or not, may please many . . .

In 1779 Betsy Flanagan set up a "tavern" near Yorktown where the American and French officers of the Revolutionary Army met and enjoyed a new sort of drink compounded by Flanagan that became very popular and was called a "bracer."

In the neighborhood, an Englishman kept splendid poultry imported from his mother country. Flanagan was fiercely hostile to this gentleman and was always promising to feed the American and French officers with a fine fowl that was in the loyalist's grounds. From time to time, they would tease her about the delay in carrying her promises into effect. One night, when there was an unusual attendance of these officers at the tavern, she invited them into her dining room where was spread a bountiful feast of chicken. The Englishman's chicken coop had been raided. When the chicken banquet was over, Flanagan invited the guests into the bar, and with great pride pointed to the chicken tails spread gracefully around bottles of "bracers." The surprise was complete, and the event recognized by three hearty cheers for Flanagan, the cause of the Colonists and confusion to the English.

The "bracers" came off those shelves in a great hurry and the remainder of the night was passed in the barroom amid the "cocks' tails" and the inspiring "bracers." "Give us some more of those Cocktails," was the frequent order; "*Vive le cocktail*," shouted a French officer. This was the keynote to the now-celebrated name. It "stuck."

The above narration may be truth or fiction; what still remains a fact that has been known for over three generations throughout the civilized world is that, by using the finest ingredients, and mixed with care and precision, the cocktail will always be the drink of good fellowship.

More and more they are becoming popular, thousands of people on every part of the globe drink them, but few have acquired the art of mixing a perfect drink. The cocktail should always be perfect: there is no reason ever to drink a bad one. Almost any of the ingredients of which cocktails are composed might better be consumed "straight" rather than just carelessly poured together.

Indications of Measures for Cocktails

2 fluid ounces 2 drams = 60 milliliters (ml);
1 fluid ounce 1 dram = 30 ml;
4½ drams = 15 ml;
3 drams = 10 ml;
2¼ drams = 75 ml or 1 teaspoon;
1 teaspoon = 6 dashes;
1 dash = about 12 drops.

No standard size of glass has so far been adopted. The measures given of the amount of liquid used to make a normal-sized cocktail are of 60 ml, or of 2 fluid ounces and 2 drams; divided into halves, fourths, eighths, etc. . . . . One-eighth equals one teaspoon or six dashes, or about 70 drops.

The "gigger"* in use in America is a very practical double measure: the bigger size holds 1 ounce 2.5 drams, or 35 milliliters; the small size about half of the abovementioned amount. The "gill," an English measure, holds 5 fluid ounces and can be divided, when mixing cocktails, in halves, thirds, fourths, fifths, sixths, eighths, etc. . . . Great care should always be taken when mixing drinks: a little too much or not quite enough of the proportions indicated often changes the entire taste, thereby spoiling the result expected.

To have a perfect blend and smoothness use only the finest ingredients in making your drinks. A cocktail is one of the last words in the artistry of mixing drinks. Follow closely the formulas given herein and choose quality brands when replenishing your supplies—aged whiskeys in Manhattans, "that supreme gin," which is "the heart of a good cocktail," in Martinis and Bronxes, and specially selected vermouths in both. Mix with infinite care and the result will be the Miracle-Cocktail which has made the Ritz Bar famous.

My book would not be complete without a word to the younger generation. Now, as in the past, the art of rational drinking is an accomplishment as indispensable as dancing or bridge, and a fair knowledge of wines and liqueurs, their provenance, characteristics, best years, etc., forms part of a gentleman's culture. The passing generation of Englishmen knew wines, and it is my sincere hope that this knowledge be increased, throughout the world.

Any young man who can convince me that his lips will never touch alcohol need not follow my required course in drinks and drinking. To know how to drink is as essential as to know how to swim, and one should be at home in both these closely related elements. Each man reacts differently to alcohol; he should know before the time when, according to custom, he indulges in his first "collegiate binge," whether

*Spelling used by Frank Meier for the jigger, a bar measuring tool.

liquor affects his head, his legs, or his morals; whether he sings, fights, weeps, climbs lampposts, or behaves with excessive affection toward the opposite sex; whether, in short, it makes him a jovial companion or a social pest. A knowledge of these weaknesses will help to overcome them.

"Know your capacity and stay within limits." One can drink sensibly, if one knows what a chaos a mixture of liquors can produce. *In vino veritas*, so often quoted, does not mean that a man will tell the truth when in drink but will reveal the hidden side of his character.

Frank Meier

"Mix with infinite care and the result will be the Miracle-Cocktail which has made the Ritz Bar famous."

2. MY FAVORITE DRINKS

Made from twelve alcoholic beverages—pastis, rum, brandy, champagne, white curaçao, gin, vermouth, port, rye whiskey, bourbon, scotch, sherry—and the following ingredients:

FRUITS: grapefruit, lemons or limes, oranges, pineapples, seasonal fruit.
GROCERIES: allspice, eggs, honey, maraschino cherries, milk, nutmeg, rock candy, salt, pepper, celery salt, sugar, tomatoes, vinegar.
MISCELLANEOUS: Angostura bitters, clam juice, fresh mint, ginger ale, soda water, Indian Tonic.
SAUCES: tabasco, tomato ketchup, Worcestershire.
SEAFOOD: crabmeat, lobster, oysters, shrimp.
SYRUPS: grenadine, lemon, pineapple, raspberry, strawberry.

196 COCKTAILS: ALPHABETICAL LIST

Absinthe n° 1, n° 2,
   & French Style
Adonis
Affinity
Alaska
Alexandra
Alexandra Special
Alfonso XIII
Almaza
Angel's Kiss
Appetiser
Applejack
Automobile
Bacardi
Bee's Kiss
Bee's Knees
Bentley
Between the Sheets
Bijou
Blackthorn
Bloodhound
Blue Bird
Bobby Burns
Boomerang
Brain Duster
Brandy
Broken Spur
Bronx
Brooklyn
Buby
Bunny Hug
Burr
B. V. D.

Byrrh
Café de Paris
Canadian
Caruso
Champagne
Champagne Pick-
   Me-Up
Chatterley
Chinese
Cider
Cinzano
Clam Juice
Clover Club
Clover Leaf
Coffee
Cora
Coronation
Corpse Reviver n° 1
Crocker
Daiquiri
Deauville
Derby
Diki-Diki
Doctor
D. O. M.
Douglas
Dubonnet
Dunlap
East India
Edward VIII
Elegant
Elk's Own
Emerald

Encore
Evans
Fascinator
Favorite
Fernet Mint
Fernet Vermouth
Fourth Degree
Frank's Special
French Vermouth
Futurity
F. Y. C. S.
Genever
Gibson
Gimlet
Gin
Gin & It
Gin & Sin
Gloom Chaser
Golden Clipper
Golden Slipper
Graves
Greenbriar
Guards
Happy Honey Annie
Harvard
Hawaiian
Highbinder
Hoffman House
Homestead
H. P. W.
H. R. W.
Ingram
Irish Whiskey

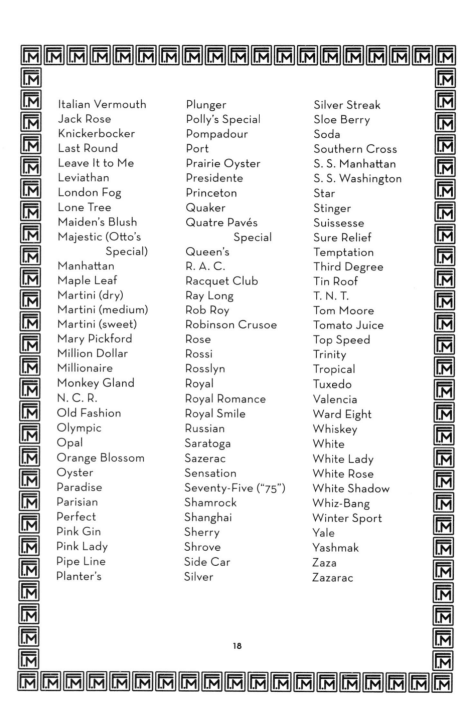

Italian Vermouth
Jack Rose
Knickerbocker
Last Round
Leave It to Me
Leviathan
London Fog
Lone Tree
Maiden's Blush
Majestic (Otto's
      Special)
Manhattan
Maple Leaf
Martini (dry)
Martini (medium)
Martini (sweet)
Mary Pickford
Million Dollar
Millionaire
Monkey Gland
N. C. R.
Old Fashion
Olympic
Opal
Orange Blossom
Oyster
Paradise
Parisian
Perfect
Pink Gin
Pink Lady
Pipe Line
Planter's

Plunger
Polly's Special
Pompadour
Port
Prairie Oyster
Presidente
Princeton
Quaker
Quatre Pavés
      Special
Queen's
R. A. C.
Racquet Club
Ray Long
Rob Roy
Robinson Crusoe
Rose
Rossi
Rosslyn
Royal
Royal Romance
Royal Smile
Russian
Saratoga
Sazerac
Sensation
Seventy-Five ("75")
Shamrock
Shanghai
Sherry
Shrove
Side Car
Silver

Silver Streak
Sloe Berry
Soda
Southern Cross
S. S. Manhattan
S. S. Washington
Star
Stinger
Suissesse
Sure Relief
Temptation
Third Degree
Tin Roof
T. N. T.
Tom Moore
Tomato Juice
Top Speed
Trinity
Tropical
Tuxedo
Valencia
Ward Eight
Whiskey
White
White Lady
White Rose
White Shadow
Whiz-Bang
Winter Sport
Yale
Yashmak
Zaza
Zazarac

233 MIXED DRINKS: DETAILED LIST

AFTER-DINNER DRINKS (2)
Angostura bitters, apricot brandy, Bénédictine.

COBBLERS (8)
Brandy, champagne, claret, port, Rhine wine, rum, Sauternes wine, sherry, whiskey.

COLLINS (2)
Brandy, gin, rum, whiskey.

COOLERS (8)
Angostura bitters, apricot brandy, brandy, gin, Irish whiskey, maraschino, rum, rye whiskey, Scotch whisky.

CRUSTAS (2)
Angostura bitters, brandy, gin, rum, whiskey.

CUPS (14)
Bénédictine, brandy, calvados (or applejack), Chablis (or Pouilly), champagne, cider, claret (or Burgundy wine), curaçao, maraschino, Moselle wine, Sauternes wine, sparkling Rhine wine, stout.

DAISIES (4)
Brandy, calvados (or applejack), gin, pastis, rum, whiskey.

EGG NOGS (3)
Bourbon, curaçao, Madeira, gin, rum, sherry, whiskey.

FIXES (2)
Brandy, curaçao, gin, rum, whiskey.

FIZZES (32)
Bacardi, brandy, champagne, cherry brandy, curaçao, Dubonnet, gin, Irish whiskey, pastis, rum, rye whiskey (or bourbon), Scotch whisky, sloe gin.

FLIPS (7)
Beer, brandy, gin, Madeira, port, rum, rye whiskey, sherry.

HIGHBALLS (2)
Brandy, gin, peach brandy, whiskey.

JULEPS (4)
Bourbon, brandy, champagne, gin, maraschino, rum, Saumur wine, whiskey.

LEMONADES (10)
Angostura bitters, brandy, claret, rum, whiskey.

PUFFS (2)
Brandy, gin, rum, whiskey.

PUNCHES (17)

Angostura bitters, apricot brandy, Bénédictine, brandy, caloric punsch, champagne, claret (or red Burgundy wine), curaçao, gin, maraschino, peach brandy, rum, rye whiskey, Sauternes.

RICKEYS (2)

Apricot brandy, brandy, gin, rum, sloe gin, whiskey.

SANGAREES (3)

Ale (porter or stout), brandy, gin, port, rum, sherry, whiskey.

SCAFFAS (4)

Angostura bitters, Bénédictine, bourbon, brandy, gin, maraschino, rum.

SHRUBS (3)

Brandy, rum, sherry.

SLINGS (3)

Angostura bitters, brandy, cherry brandy, gin, rum, whiskey.

SMASHES (2)

Brandy, gin, rum, whiskey.

SOURS (2)

Brandy, calvados (or applejack), gin, rum, whiskey.

TODDIES (2)

Brandy, calvados (or applejack), gin, peach brandy, rum, whiskey.

ZOOMS (2)

Brandy, gin, rum, whiskey.

HOT DRINKS (22)

Angostura bitters, brandy, calvados (or applejack), curaçao, claret, gin, peach brandy, port, red wine, rum, Scotch whisky, sherry, whiskey.

MISCELLANEOUS DRINKS (59)

Absinthe, Amer Picon, Angostura bitters, Bordeaux wine, bourbon, brandy, Byrrh, Campari, champagne, Chartreuse, cognac, créme de cassis, créme de menthe, curaçao, Danziger Goldwasser, Dubonnet, French vermouth, gin, Guinness, Irish whiskey, Italian vermouth, kirsch, kümmel, Madeira, maraschino, pale ale, pastis, peach brandy, port, Rhine wine (or Moselle wine), rum, rye whiskey, Scotch whisky, sherry, stout.

NONALCOHOLIC DRINKS (10)

Chocolate, clam juice, coffee, grape, grenadine, lemon, milk, orgeat, strawberry, tea.

3. VARIOUS SPECIALTIES & THEIR ORIGINS

AGUARDIENTE: a strong liquor distilled from grapes; popular in Spain and Mexico.

AKVAVIT: a strong white liqueur made in Scandinavia.

ARACK, GUARUZO, & KAMTCHATKA WATKY: beverages distilled from rice.

ARAKI & LAGBI: liquors made from the juice of dates.

BARACK-PALINKA: a Hungarian liquor distilled from apricots.

CACHIRI & PRAYA: beverages made from sweet potatoes.

CALISAY: a Magenbitter (herbal liqueur) made in Freiburg, Germany.

CANA, CAXACA, GUARAPO, PARATY, & TEQUILA: beverages distilled from sugarcane.

CHA & SINDAY: beverages made in China and India from the sap of the palm tree.

CHICHA: a Bolivian beverage distilled from grapes.

DANTZIGER GOLDWASSER: a delicious white liqueur containing little gold flakes.

DOUZICO: absinthe made in Turkey.

ÉLIXIR DE SPA: a beverage considered the best cure for indigestion.

FINKEL: a lower-quality gin made in Norway.

FUNDADOR: the name of a Spanish brandy.

IVA LIQUEUR: a green liqueur obtained from herbs grown on the highest Alps in Switzerland.

IZARRA: one of the many French liqueurs (like Chartreuse, Bénédictine, Florestine des Alpes, or Vieille Cure).

KAWA: made from certain roots in Hawaii.

KIRSCHWASSER: an eau-de-vie distilled from cherries.

KVAS: a national beverage in Russia, made from bread.

MARASCHINO: distilled from the bitter Mahaleb cherry.

MASTIC: a liqueur made in Greece.

MAZATO: a Peruvian beverage made from corn.

MESCAL: a Mexican liquor made from Maquey aloe.

MONTWIJN: Old Dutch word for whiskey.

NALIVKA: a liqueur very popular in Russia.

OAKULIHOU: a popular beverage in the Hawaiian Islands.

PIMENTO DRAM: a variety of rum made in Jamaica.

PINCHE SOTO: a liqueur made in Spain.

POLYNNAIA: a sort of whiskey made in Russia.

POTHEEN: name given to whiskey distilled privately in Ireland.

QUETSCH OR SLIVOVITZ: a beverage distilled from prunes (very popular in Central Europe and the Balkans).

RATAFIA: a liqueur made from different fruits or plants macerated in alcohol.

SAKE: made from rice and the national drink in Japan.

SBITEN: a hot drink popular in northern Russia made with honey, pepper, and boiling water.

SCHNAPPS: Holland gin, originally made in Schiedam; the word "Schnapps" is commonly used in Europe to designate potent spirits of all sorts.

SPUMANTE: Italian term for sparkling wines.

TAFIA: an inferior type of rum made from molasses.

TUICA: a prune liquor made in Romania.

UCHI: an African beverage made from fermented coconuts, wild dates, and other similar fruits.

ULPO: a popular Chilean beverage made from roasted wheat.

URUK: a beverage distilled from wild apricot and cherry in Siberia.

USQUEBAUGH (IRISH); UISGEBEATHA (CELTIC): the first words used to describe whiskey.

USUPH: a wine made in Morocco.

VAN DER HUM: an elixir made in South Africa.

VODKA: a very popular drink in Russia distilled from grains.

WACHHOLDER: distilled from juniper.

YAWA: a palm wine very popular in West Africa.

YWERA: a type of whiskey made in the Sandwich Islands.

ZYTHUS: a Syrian beverage made from fermented flour.

Recipes with the symbol ◈ were created by Frank Meier.

I.
COCKTAILS

"Thirsty earth drinks up the rain,
Trees from earth drink that again;
Ocean drinks the air; the sun
Drinks the sea. And him the moon.
Any reason, canst thou think,
I should thirst while all these drink?"
Anacreon*

*Translated by William Hand Browne in Jakob Von Falke's *Greece and Rome* (1886).

WHAT WOULD A DINNER BE WITHOUT A COCKTAIL?

In mixing cocktails or any other drinks, whether in a shaker or mixing glass, ice always precedes the other ingredients.

The term "glass" used throughout these recipes means a two-ounce (60 ml) glass. The designations "one-fifth," "one-sixth," etc., not followed by the word "glass" indicate fractional parts of the liquor or ingredient used.

ABSINTHE n° 1
In a shaker: a dash (⅛ tsp/.5 ml) of anisette, one glass (2 oz/60 ml) of absinthe; shake well and serve very cold.

ABSINTHE n° 2
In a shaker: a dash (⅛ tsp/.5 ml) of orange bitters, one-third (¾ oz/22 ml) gin, two-thirds (1¼ oz/37 ml) absinthe; shake well and serve very cold. Add sugar or syrup if absinthe is not sweetened.

ABSINTHE (French Style)
In a tumbler: a large piece of ice, one glass (2 oz/60 ml) of absinthe; place a lump of sugar on an absinthe spoon or a fork, pour water over it to suit taste, and serve.

ADONIS
In a mixing glass: a dash (⅛ tsp/.5 ml) of orange bitters, half (1 oz/30 ml) dry sherry, half (1 oz/30 ml) Italian vermouth; stir slightly and serve.

AFFINITY
In a mixing glass: a dash (⅛ tsp/.5 ml) of Angostura bitters, one-fourth each (½ oz/15 ml) of French and Italian vermouth, half (1 oz/30 ml) Scotch whisky; stir well and serve.

ALASKA
In a shaker: one-third (¾ oz/22 ml) yellow Chartreuse, two-thirds (1¼ oz/37 ml) gin; shake well and serve.

ALEXANDRA

In a shaker: one-fourth (½ oz/ 15 ml) each heavy cream and crème de cacao, half (1 oz/30 ml) gin; shake well and serve.

ALEXANDRA SPECIAL

In a shaker: one-fourth (½ oz/ 15 ml) each heavy cream and anisette, half (1 oz/30 ml) brandy; shake well and serve.

ALFONSO XIII   ❖

In a mixing glass: half (1 oz/30 ml) Dubonnet, half (1 oz/30 ml) dry sherry; stir slightly and serve.

ALMAZA

In a mixing glass: a teaspoon (5 ml) of Aperitivo Rossi, two-thirds (1¼ oz/ 37 ml) gin; one-third (¾ oz/22 ml) Martini vermouth; stir well and serve.

ANGEL'S KISS

In a liqueur glass: pour slowly and carefully one-third (¾ oz/22 ml) each of crème de cacao, brandy, and heavy cream. Ingredients should not mix.

APPETISER

In a mixing glass: a teaspoon (5 ml) of maraschino, a dash (⅛ tsp/ .5 ml) of Angostura bitters, one glass (2 oz/60 ml) of brandy; stir well and serve.

APPLEJACK

In a shaker: a dash (⅛ tsp/.5 ml) of orange bitters, a teaspoon (5 ml) of curaçao, one glass (2 oz/60 ml) of applejack (or calvados); shake well and serve.

AUTOMOBILE

In a mixing glass: a dash (⅛ tsp/ .5 ml) of orange bitters, one-third (1 oz/30 ml) each of Italian vermouth, gin, and Scotch whisky; stir well and serve.

BACARDI

In a shaker: the juice of a quarter lemon, a teaspoon (5 ml) of French vermouth, half a teaspoon (2.5 ml) of grenadine, half a glass (1 oz/30 ml) of Bacardi rum; shake well and serve.

BEE'S KISS

In a shaker: a teaspoon (5 ml) each of heavy cream and honey, half a glass (1 oz/30 ml) of rum; shake well and serve.

BEE'S KNEES

In a shaker: the juice of a quarter lemon, a teaspoon (5 ml) of honey, half a glass (1 oz/30 ml) of gin; shake well and serve.

BENTLEY

In a mixing glass: half (1 oz/ 30 ml) Dubonnet, half (1 oz/30 ml) applejack (or calvados); stir well and serve.

BETWEEN THE SHEETS

In a shaker: a teaspoon (5 ml) of lemon juice, one-third (1 oz/30 ml) each of brandy, curaçao, and rum; shake well and serve.

BIJOU

In a mixing glass: a dash (1/8 tsp/ .5 ml) of orange bitters, one-third (1 oz/30 ml) each of French vermouth, curaçao, and gin; stir well and serve with a maraschino cherry.

BLACKTHORN

In a mixing glass: a dash (1/8 tsp/ .5 ml) each of Angostura bitters and pastis, half (1 oz/30 ml) French vermouth, half (1 oz/30 ml) Irish whiskey; stir well and serve.

BLOODHOUND

In a shaker: crush three ripe strawberries, add a teaspoon (5 ml) each of French and Italian vermouth, half a glass (1 oz/30 ml) of gin; shake well and serve.

BLUE BIRD

Special for Sir Malcolm Campbell.*
In a shaker: a teaspoon (5 ml) each of lemon juice and curaçao, half a glass (1 oz/30 ml) of gin, three drops of blue food coloring; shake well and serve.

*This cocktail was created in 1927 by Frank Meier to celebrate the new automobile speed record set by Sir Malcolm Campbell in his Blue Bird—he reached a speed of over 173 mph (280 km/h).

BOBBY BURNS

In a mixing glass: a dash (1/8 tsp/.5 ml) of Bénédictine, one-fourth (1/2 oz/15 ml) each of Italian and French vermouth, half (1 oz/30 ml) Scotch whisky; stir well and serve.

BOOMERANG

In a shaker: a dash (1/8 tsp/.5 ml) of Angostura bitters, one-third (1 oz/30 ml) each of French vermouth, Scotch whisky, and Swedish punsch; shake well and serve.

BRAIN DUSTER

In a shaker: the juice of half a lemon, one glass (2 oz/60 ml) of anise liqueur, two teaspoons (10 ml) of dry sherry; shake well, strain into a double cocktail glass, and serve.

BRANDY

In a mixing glass: a dash (1/8 tsp/.5 ml) of Angostura bitters, two dashes (1/4 tsp/1 ml) of Italian vermouth, one glass (2 oz/60 ml) of brandy; stir well and serve.

BROKEN SPUR

In a shaker: one egg yolk, a dash (1/8 tsp/.5 ml) of anisette, half a glass (1 oz/30 ml) each of gin and white port; shake well, strain into a double cocktail glass, and serve with grated nutmeg.

BRONX

In a shaker: squeeze a slice or one-eighth of an orange, one-fourth (1/2 oz/15 ml) each of French and Italian vermouth, half (1 oz/30 ml) gin; shake well and serve.

BROOKLYN

In a mixing glass: a dash (1/8 tsp/.5 ml) of maraschino, half (1 oz/30 ml) French vermouth, half (1 oz/30 ml) rye whiskey; stir well and serve.

BUBY

Special for Mr. F. Worthington Hine.

In a shaker: a teaspoon (5 ml) of grenadine, half (1 oz/30 ml) lemon juice, half (1 oz/30 ml) gin; shake well and serve.

BUNNY HUG

In a shaker: one-third (1 oz/30 ml) each of gin, Scotch whisky, and sweetened pastis; shake well and serve.

BURR

Special for Mr. H. Courtney Burr.

In a shaker: one-fifth (1/2 oz/15 ml) Martini vermouth, four-fifths (2 oz/60 ml) Plymouth gin; shake well and serve.

B. V. D.

In a mixing glass: one-third (1 oz/30 ml) each of **B**acardi rum, **V**ermouth (French), and **D**ubonnet; stir well and serve.

BYRRH

In a mixing glass: one-sixth (½ oz/15 ml) kirsch, two-sixths (1 oz/30 ml) brandy, half (1 ½ oz/45 ml) Byrrh; shake well and serve.

CAFÉ DE PARIS

In a shaker: half an egg white, a dash (⅛ tsp/.5 ml) of anisette, a teaspoon (5 ml) of heavy cream, half a glass (1 oz/30 ml) of gin; shake well, strain into a double cocktail glass, and serve.

CANADIAN

In a mixing glass: a dash (⅛ tsp/.5 ml) of Angostura bitters, two-thirds (1 ¼ oz/37 ml) Canadian whisky, one-third (¾ oz/22 ml) Italian vermouth; stir well and serve.

CARUSO

In a mixing glass: one-third (1 oz/30 ml) each of French vermouth, St. Raphael, and gin; stir well and serve.

CHAMPAGNE

In a large wineglass: a dash (⅛ tsp/.5 ml) of Angostura bitters on a small lump of sugar, a slice of lemon peel, a piece of ice; fill with champagne, stir, and serve.

CHAMPAGNE PICK-ME-UP

In a shaker: a dash (⅛ tsp/.5 ml) of grenadine, the juice of half an orange, half a glass (1 oz/30 ml) of brandy; shake well, strain into a fizz glass, fill with champagne, and serve.

CHATTERLEY

In a shaker: a teaspoon (5 ml) each of orange juice and curaçao, one-fourth (½ oz/15 ml) French vermouth, half (1 oz/30 ml) gin; shake well and serve.

CHINESE

In a shaker: a dash (⅛ tsp/.5 ml) each of Angostura bitters and maraschino, a teaspoon (5 ml) of grenadine, half a glass (1 oz/30 ml) of rum; shake well and serve.

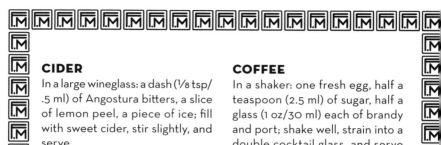

CIDER

In a large wineglass: a dash (1/8 tsp/ .5 ml) of Angostura bitters, a slice of lemon peel, a piece of ice; fill with sweet cider, stir slightly, and serve.

CINZANO

In a mixing glass: a dash (1/8 tsp/ .5 ml) each of Angostura bitters and orange bitters, one glass (2 oz/60 ml) of Cinzano vermouth; stir and serve with orange or lemon peel.

CLAM JUICE

In a shaker: a teaspoon (5 ml) of ketchup, a small pinch of celery salt, two or three drops of Tabasco sauce, half a glass (1 oz/30 ml) of clam juice; shake slightly and serve.

CLOVER CLUB

In a shaker: half an egg white, the juice of half a lemon, a teaspoon (5 ml) of grenadine, one glass (2 oz/60 ml) of gin; shake well, strain into a small wineglass, and serve.

CLOVER LEAF

The same as Clover Club; add a few sprigs of fresh mint.

COFFEE

In a shaker: one fresh egg, half a teaspoon (2.5 ml) of sugar, half a glass (1 oz/30 ml) each of brandy and port; shake well, strain into a double cocktail glass, and serve with grated nutmeg if desired. The name of this drink is derived from its color; it does not contain any coffee.

CORA

In a mixing glass: a dash (1/8 tsp/ 5 ml) of orange bitters, half (1 oz/30 ml) brandy, half (1 oz/30 ml) Cora vermouth; stir well and serve.

CORONATION

In a mixing glass: a dash (1/8 tsp/ .5 ml) of maraschino, a dash (1/8 tsp/.5 ml) of orange bitters, half (1 oz/30 ml) French vermouth, half (1 oz/30 ml) dry sherry; stir slightly and serve.

CORPSE REVIVER N° 1

In a shaker: one-third (1 oz/30 ml) each of Italian vermouth, apple-jack (or calvados), and brandy; shake well and serve.

See Corpse Reviver n° 2 on page 106

CROCKER ❖

Special for Mr. W. W. Crocker.

In a shaker: a dash (1/8 tsp/.5 ml) of French vermouth, a dash (1/8 tsp/ .5 ml) of Italian vermouth, four-fifths (2 oz/60 ml) gin; shake well and serve very cold.

DAIQUIRI

In a shaker: the juice of half a lime or a quarter lemon, half a teaspoon (2.5 ml) of sugar, half a glass (1 oz/30 ml) of rum; shake well and serve.

DEAUVILLE

In a large wineglass: a dash (1/8 tsp/.5 ml) of Angostura bitters on a small lump of sugar, a dash (1/8 tsp/.5 ml) of pastis, a piece of ice; fill with champagne, add a dash (1/8 tsp/.5 ml) of applejack (or calvados) on top, and serve.

DERBY

In a shaker: a dash (1/8 tsp/.5 ml) of peach bitters, a sprig of fresh mint, one glass (2 oz/60 ml) of gin; shake well and serve.

DIKI-DIKI

In a shaker: one-sixth (1/2 oz/15 ml) unsweetened grapefruit juice, one-sixth (1/2 oz/15 ml) Swedish punsch, two-thirds (2 oz/60 ml) applejack (or calvados); shake well and serve.

DOCTOR

In a shaker: a teaspoon (5 ml) each of lemon and orange juice, half (1 oz/30 ml) Swedish punsch, half (1 oz/30 ml) rum; shake well and serve.

D. O. M.

In a shaker: a teaspoon (5 ml) each of orange juice and Bénédictine, three-fourths (1 oz/45 ml) gin; shake well and serve.

DOUGLAS

In a mixing glass: one-third (3/4 oz/ 22 ml) French vermouth, two-thirds (1 1/4 oz/37 ml) Old Tom gin; stir well and serve with an orange peel.

DUBONNET

In a mixing glass: a dash (1/8 tsp/ .5 ml) of Angostura bitters, one glass (2 oz/60 ml) of Dubonnet; stir slightly and serve with a lemon peel.

DUNLAP

In a mixing glass: a dash (1/8 tsp/ .5 ml) of Angostura bitters, half (1 oz/30 ml) sweet sherry, half (1 oz/30 ml) rum; stir well and serve.

EAST INDIA

In a shaker: a dash (⅛ tsp/.5 ml) of Angostura bitters, a teaspoon (5 ml) of pineapple syrup, one glass (2 oz/60 ml) of brandy; shake well and serve with a piece of pineapple.

EDWARD VIII ◈

In a small tumbler: one glass (2 oz/60 ml) of Seagram's rye whiskey, a dash (⅛ tsp/.5 ml) of pastis, two teaspoons (10 ml) each of Italian vermouth and plain water, a piece of ice in a long orange peel; stir well and serve.

ELEGANT ◈

In a mixing glass; a dash (⅛ tsp/.5 ml) of Grand Marnier, half (1 oz/30 ml) French vermouth, half (1 oz/30 ml) gin; stir well and serve.

ELK'S OWN

In a shaker: half an egg white, a teaspoon (5 ml) of lemon juice, half a teaspoon (2.5 ml) of sugar, half a glass (1 oz/30 ml) each of port and Canadian whisky; shake well, strain into a small wineglass, and serve.

EMERALD

In a shaker: half (1 oz/30 ml) Prunellia, half (1 oz/30 ml) gin; shake well and serve. An after-dinner drink.

ENCORE

In a pousse-café glass: pour slowly on top of one another one-third (1 oz/30 ml) each of curaçao, maraschino, and brandy; set aflame, allow to burn for one minute, let glass cool, and serve. An after-dinner drink.

EVANS

Special for Mr. Montgomery Evans.*
In a mixing glass: a dash (⅛ tsp/.5 ml) each of apricot brandy and curaçao, one glass (2 oz/60 ml) of rye whiskey; stir well and serve.

*The American writer and world traveler.

FASCINATOR

In a shaker: a dash (⅛ tsp/.5 ml) of pastis, half (1 oz/30 ml) French vermouth, half (1 oz/30 ml) gin, a sprig of mint; shake well and serve.

FAVORITE

In a mixing glass: one-third (1 oz/ 30 ml) each of French vermouth, apricot brandy, and gin, a dash (⅛ tsp/.5 ml) of lime or lemon juice; stir well and serve.

FERNET MINT

In a cocktail glass: half (1 oz/30 ml) Fernet-Branca, half (1 oz/30 ml) green crème de menthe; stir slightly and serve. May be iced if desired.

FERNET VERMOUTH

In a cocktail glass: half (1 oz/30 ml) Fernet-Branca, half (1 oz/30 ml) Italian vermouth; stir slightly and serve. May be served iced if desired.

FOURTH DEGREE

In a mixing glass: two dashes (¼ tsp/1 ml) of pastis, one-fourth (½ oz/15 ml) French vermouth, one-fourth (½ oz/15 ml) Italian vermouth, half (1 oz/30 ml) gin; stir well and serve.

FRANK'S SPECIAL

In a mixing glass: a dash (⅛ tsp/ .5 ml) of peach brandy, half (1 oz/30 ml) French vermouth, half (1 oz/30 ml) Gordon's gin; stir well and serve.

FRENCH VERMOUTH

In a mixing glass: a dash (⅛ tsp/.5 ml) each of orange bitters and curaçao, one glass (2 oz/60 ml) of French vermouth; stir slightly and serve.

FUTURITY

In a mixing glass: a dash (⅛ tsp/ .5 ml) of Angostura bitters, one-third (¾ oz/22 ml) French vermouth, two-thirds (1 ¼ oz/ 37 ml) sloe gin; stir well and serve.

F. Y. C. S.
(Florida Yacht Club Special)

In a shaker: a teaspoon (5 ml) each of French and Italian vermouth, two teaspoons (10 ml) of unsweetened grapefruit juice, half a glass (1 oz/30 ml) of rum; shake well, strain into a small wineglass containing a piece of ice, and serve.

GENEVER

In a mixing glass: a dash (1/8 tsp/ .5 ml) of Angostura bitters, one glass (2 oz/60 ml) of Holland gin; stir well and serve.

GIBSON

In a mixing glass: one-fourth (1/2 oz/ 15 ml) Italian vermouth, three-fourths (1 oz/45 ml) gin; stir well and serve with a small white onion.

GIMLET

In a cocktail glass: one-third (3/4 oz/22 ml) lime juice cordial, two-thirds (1 1/4 oz/37 ml) gin; stir and serve. Do not serve iced.

GIN

In a mixing glass: a dash (1/8 tsp/ .5 ml) of Angostura bitters, a dash (1/8 tsp/.5 ml) of Italian vermouth, one glass (2 oz/60 ml) of gin; stir well and serve.

GIN & IT (Gin & Italian)

In a cocktail glass: half (1 oz/ 30 ml) gin, half (1 oz/30 ml) Italian vermouth. Do not serve iced.

GIN & SIN

In a shaker: a dash (1/8 tsp/.5 ml) of grenadine, a teaspoon (5 ml) each of orange and lemon juice, three-fourths (1 oz/45 ml) gin; shake well and serve.

GLOOM CHASER

In a shaker: a teaspoon (5 ml) of curaçao, the juice of a quarter lemon, half a glass (1 oz/30 ml) of rum; shake well and serve.

GOLDEN CLIPPER

In a shaker: one-fourth (1/2 oz/ 15 ml) each of orange juice, peach brandy, rum, and gin; shake well and serve.

GOLDEN SLIPPER

In a cocktail glass: one-third (3/4 oz/ 22 ml) Bénédictine, one egg yolk, one-third (3/4 oz/22 ml) Dantziger Goldwasser. Ingredients should not mix.

GRAVES

In a mixing glass: one-sixth (1/2 oz/ 15 ml) each of French and Martini vermouth, two-thirds (2 oz/60 ml) yellow gin; stir well and serve.

GREENBRIAR

In a shaker: a dash (1/8 tsp/.5 ml) of peach bitters, half (1 oz/30 ml) French vermouth, half (1 oz/30 ml) sweet sherry, a sprig of fresh mint; shake slightly and serve.

GUARDS

In a mixing glass: a dash (1/8 tsp/ .5 ml) of curaçao, one-third (3/4 oz/ 22 ml) Italian vermouth, two-thirds (1 1/4 oz/37 ml) gin; shake well and serve.

HAPPY HONEY ANNIE

Special for Mr. P. A. Chavannes.*
In a shaker: half a teaspoon (2.5 ml) of honey, one-third (3/4 oz/ 22 ml) unsweetened grapefruit juice, two-thirds (1 1/4 oz/37 ml) brandy; shake well and serve.

HARVARD

In mixing glass: a dash (1/8 tsp/.5 ml) of Angostura bitters, half (1 oz/30 ml) Italian vermouth, half (1 oz/ 30 ml) brandy; stir well and serve.

HAWAIIAN

In a shaker: a dash (1/8 tsp/.5 ml) of curaçao, the juice of a quarter orange, half a glass (1 oz/30 ml) of gin; shake well and serve.

HIGHBINDER

In a cocktail glass: half (1 oz/30 ml) brandy, half (1 oz/30 ml) blackberry liqueur; stir and serve.

HOFFMAN HOUSE

In a mixing glass: a dash (1/8 tsp/ .5 ml) of orange bitters, one-third (3/4 oz/22 ml) French vermouth, two-thirds (1 1/4 oz/37 ml) Old Tom gin; stir well and serve with orange peel.

HOMESTEAD

In a shaker: a slice of orange, one-third (3/4 oz/22 ml) Italian vermouth, two-thirds (1 1/4 oz/ 37 ml) gin; shake well and serve.

H. P. W.

In a mixing glass: half (1 oz/30 ml) Italian Vermouth, half (1 oz/ 30 ml) gin; stir well and serve with an orange peel.

H. R. W.

In a shaker: crush three or four very ripe cherries, add one-third (3/4 oz/22 ml) French vermouth, two-thirds (1 1/4 oz/37 ml) gin; shake well and serve.

INGRAM

In a shaker: a dash (1/8 tsp/.5 ml) of grenadine, half (1 oz/30 ml) orange juice, half (1 oz/30 ml) lemon juice; shake slightly and serve.

*Pierre-André Chavannes, a member of the French Resistance, was arrested during the Nazi Occupation, and it was thanks to this cocktail book that he was saved. After the Nazi soldiers saw Frank Meier's book (which they knew) at Chavannes' place, Chavannes offered them a cocktail. Delighted, they drank more than they should have and Chavannes took the opportunity to slip away!

IRISH WHISKEY

In mixing glass: a dash (⅛ tsp/ .5 ml) each of Angostura bitters, curaçao, maraschino, and pastis, then three-fourths (1 oz/45 ml) Irish whiskey; stir well and serve.

ITALIAN VERMOUTH

In mixing glass: a dash (⅛ tsp/ .5 ml) of Angostura bitters, one glass (2 oz/60 ml) of Martini-Rossi vermouth; stir well and serve.

JACK ROSE

In a shaker: the juice of a quarter lemon, half a teaspoon (5 ml) of grenadine, half a glass (1 oz/30 ml) of applejack (or calvados); shake well and serve.

KNICKERBOCKER

In a shaker: crush a small slice of ripe pineapple, a teaspoon (5 ml) each of raspberry syrup, lemon juice, and orange juice, then one glass (2 oz/60 ml) of rum; shake well, strain into a small wineglass, and serve.

LAST ROUND

In a mixing glass: two dashes (¼ oz/ 1 ml) of pastis, two dashes (¼ oz/ 1 ml) of brandy, half (1 oz/30 ml) French vermouth, half (1 oz/30 ml) gin; stir well and serve.

LEAVE IT TO ME

In a shaker: a teaspoon (5 ml) of lemon juice, a dash (⅛ tsp/.5 ml) of maraschino, one-fourth (½ oz/ 15 ml) each of apricot brandy and French vermouth, half (1 oz/30 ml) gin; shake well and serve.

LEVIATHAN

In a shaker: one-fourth (½ oz/ 15 ml) orange juice, one-fourth (½ oz/15 ml) Italian vermouth, half (1 oz/30 ml) brandy; shake well and serve.

LONDON FOG

In a shaker: a dash (⅛ tsp/.5 ml) of Angostura bitters, half (1 oz/ 30 ml) white crème de menthe, half (1 oz/30 ml) anisette; shake well and serve. An after-dinner drink.

LONE TREE

In a mixing glass: one-third (¾ oz/ 22 ml) Italian vermouth, two-thirds (1 ¼ oz/37 ml) gin; stir well and serve with an olive.

MAIDEN'S BLUSH

In a shaker: half a teaspoon (2.5 ml) of grenadine, one-third (¾ oz/22 ml) pastis, two-thirds (1 ¼ oz/37 ml) gin; shake well and serve.

MAJESTIC (OTTO'S SPECIAL)

In a shaker: the juice of half a lemon, a teaspoon (5 ml) each of French and Italian vermouth, one glass (2 oz/60 ml) of white rum; shake well, strain into a double cocktail glass, and serve.

MANHATTAN

In a mixing glass: one-fourth (½ oz/15 ml) Italian vermouth, one-fourth (½ oz/15 ml) French vermouth, half (1 oz/30 ml) rye whiskey; stir well and serve.

MAPLE LEAF

In a shaker: the juice of half a lemon, half a glass (1 oz/30 ml) of bourbon whiskey, a teaspoon (5 ml) of maple syrup; shake well and serve.

MARTINI (dry)

In a mixing glass: half (1 oz/30 ml) French vermouth, half (1 oz/30 ml) gin; stir well and serve.

MARTINI (medium)

In a mixing glass: one-fourth (½ oz/15 ml) French vermouth, one-fourth (½ oz/15 ml) Martini vermouth, half (1 oz/30 ml) gin; stir well and serve.

MARTINI (sweet)

In a mixing glass: half (1 oz/30 ml) Martini vermouth, half (1 oz/30 ml) gin; stir well and serve.

MARY PICKFORD

In a shaker: half a teaspoon (2.5 ml) of grenadine, half (1 oz/30 ml) unsweetened pineapple juice, half (1 oz/30 ml) white rum; shake well and serve.

MILLION DOLLAR

In a shaker: half an egg white, a dash (⅛ tsp/.5 ml) of grenadine, a teaspoon (5 ml) of pineapple juice, half a glass (1 oz/30 ml) of gin; shake well, strain into a double cocktail glass, and serve.

MILLIONAIRE

In a shaker: half an egg white, a dash (⅛ tsp/.5 ml) of pastis, a dash (⅛ tsp/.5 ml) of grenadine, half a glass (1 oz/30 ml) of rye whiskey; shake well, strain into a double cocktail glass, and serve.

MONKEY GLAND

In a shaker: a dash (1/8 tsp/.5 ml) of pastis, a dash (1/8 tsp/.5 ml) of grenadine, half (1 oz/30 ml) orange juice, half (1 oz/30 ml) gin; shake well and serve.

N. C. R. ◈

Special for the National Cash Register Company.

In a shaker: one-third (1 oz/30 ml) each of Noilly Prat vermouth, crème de Cacao, and Rum; shake well and serve.

OLD FASHION

In a small tumbler: a dash (1/8 tsp/.5 ml) of Angostura bitters on a small lump of sugar, enough water to dissolve the sugar, one glass (2 oz/60 ml) of rye or bourbon whiskey, a large piece of ice; stir, add half a slice of orange, and serve with a glass of water. This is the old-fashioned way of making cocktails. Any liquor may be chosen to replace whiskey.

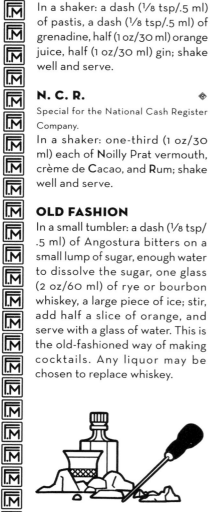

OLYMPIC ◈

In a shaker: one-fourth (1/2 oz/15 ml) each of curaçao and orange juice, half (1 oz/30 ml) brandy; shake well and serve.

OPAL

In a mixing glass: one-third (1 oz/30 ml) each of pastis, French vermouth, and gin; stir well and serve.

ORANGE BLOSSOM

In a shaker: half (1 oz/30 ml) orange juice, half (1 oz/30 ml) gin; shake well and serve. Grenadine may be added if desired.

OYSTER

In a wineglass: a tablespoon (15 ml) of ketchup, a teaspoon (5 ml) of lemon juice or chili vinegar, a little salt and pepper, a few drops of Worcestershire and Tabasco sauces. Remove four to six fat oysters from their shells, placing them in a glass containing the above mixture; stir and serve. Crab, lobster, or shrimp can be used instead of oysters.

PARADISE

In a shaker: one-fourth (1/2 oz/15 ml) each of orange juice and apricot brandy, half (1 oz/30 ml) gin; shake well and serve.

PARISIAN

In a mixing glass: a teaspoon (5 ml) of crème de cassis, half (1 oz/ 30 ml) French vermouth, half (1 oz/ 30 ml) gin; stir well and serve.

PERFECT

In a mixing glass: one-fourth (½ oz/ 15 ml) each of French and Italian vermouth, half (1 oz/30 ml) gin; stir well and serve with orange peel.

PINK GIN

In a small wineglass: two dashes (¼ tsp/1 ml) of Angostura bitters, one glass (2 oz/60 ml) of gin; a little ice water may be added if desired.

PINK LADY

In a shaker: half an egg white, a teaspoon (5 ml) each of grenadine, lemon juice, and brandy, half a glass (1 oz/30 ml) of gin; strain into a double cocktail glass and serve.

PIPE LINE

In a shaker: one-fourth (½ oz/15 ml) lemon juice, one-fourth (½ oz/15 ml) apricot brandy, half (1 oz/30 ml) rum; shake well and serve.

PLANTER'S

In a shaker: one-fourth (½ oz/ 15 ml) lemon syrup, one-fourth (½ oz/15 ml) orange juice, half (1 oz/30 ml) rum; shake well and serve.

PLUNGER

A favorite at the casinos in Deauville and Cannes. In a shaker: one-third (1 oz/30 ml) each of Swedish punsch, rum, and apple-jack (or calvados); shake well and serve.

POLLY'S SPECIAL

By W. Pollock, Park Lane Hotel, London. In a shaker: one-fourth (½ oz/ 15 ml) each of unsweetened grapefruit juice and curaçao, half (1 oz/30 ml) Scotch whisky; shake well and serve.

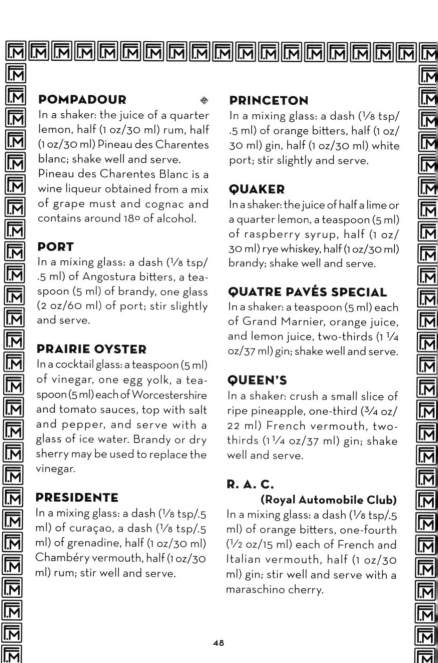

POMPADOUR

In a shaker: the juice of a quarter lemon, half (1 oz/30 ml) rum, half (1 oz/30 ml) Pineau des Charentes blanc; shake well and serve.

Pineau des Charentes Blanc is a wine liqueur obtained from a mix of grape must and cognac and contains around 18º of alcohol.

PORT

In a mixing glass: a dash (⅛ tsp/.5 ml) of Angostura bitters, a teaspoon (5 ml) of brandy, one glass (2 oz/60 ml) of port; stir slightly and serve.

PRAIRIE OYSTER

In a cocktail glass: a teaspoon (5 ml) of vinegar, one egg yolk, a teaspoon (5 ml) each of Worcestershire and tomato sauces, top with salt and pepper, and serve with a glass of ice water. Brandy or dry sherry may be used to replace the vinegar.

PRESIDENTE

In a mixing glass: a dash (⅛ tsp/.5 ml) of curaçao, a dash (⅛ tsp/.5 ml) of grenadine, half (1 oz/30 ml) Chambéry vermouth, half (1 oz/30 ml) rum; stir well and serve.

PRINCETON

In a mixing glass: a dash (⅛ tsp/.5 ml) of orange bitters, half (1 oz/30 ml) gin, half (1 oz/30 ml) white port; stir slightly and serve.

QUAKER

In a shaker: the juice of half a lime or a quarter lemon, a teaspoon (5 ml) of raspberry syrup, half (1 oz/30 ml) rye whiskey, half (1 oz/30 ml) brandy; shake well and serve.

QUATRE PAVÉS SPECIAL

In a shaker: a teaspoon (5 ml) each of Grand Marnier, orange juice, and lemon juice, two-thirds (1 ¼ oz/37 ml) gin; shake well and serve.

QUEEN'S

In a shaker: crush a small slice of ripe pineapple, one-third (¾ oz/22 ml) French vermouth, two-thirds (1 ¼ oz/37 ml) gin; shake well and serve.

R. A. C.
(Royal Automobile Club)

In a mixing glass: a dash (⅛ tsp/.5 ml) of orange bitters, one-fourth (½ oz/15 ml) each of French and Italian vermouth, half (1 oz/30 ml) gin; stir well and serve with a maraschino cherry.

RACQUET CLUB

In a mixing glass: a dash (1/8 tsp/ .5 ml) of orange bitters, one-third (3/4 oz/22 ml) French vermouth, two-thirds (1 1/4 oz/37 ml) gin; stir well and serve.

RAY LONG

In a mixing glass: a dash (1/8 tsp/.5 ml) of Angostura bitters, a dash (1/8 tsp/.5 ml) of pastis, one-third (3/4 oz/22 ml) Italian vermouth, two-thirds (1 1/4 oz/37 ml) brandy; stir well and serve.

ROB ROY

In a mixing glass: a dash (1/8 tsp/.5 ml) of Angostura bitters, one-third (3/4 oz/22 ml) Italian vermouth, two-thirds (1 1/4 oz/37 ml) Scotch whisky; stir well and serve.

ROBINSON CRUSOE

In a coconut shell containing a piece of ice: half (1 oz/30 ml) pineapple juice, half (1 oz/30 ml) rum; stir and serve.

ROSE

This cocktail, famous in Paris, was invented by "Johnny" Mitta of the Chatham Bar.
In a mixing glass: a teaspoon (5 ml) of raspberry syrup, one-third (3/4 oz/22 ml) kirsch, two-thirds (1 1/4 oz/ 37 ml) French vermouth, stir well and serve with a maraschino cherry.

ROSSI

In a mixing glass: a dash (1/8 tsp/ .5 ml) of orange bitters, half (1 oz/ 30 ml) Aperitif Rossi, half (1 oz/ 30 ml) gin; stir well and serve.

ROSSLYN

In a mixing glass: a dash (1/8 tsp/ .5 ml) of grenadine, two-thirds (1 1/4 oz/37 ml) gin, one-third (3/4 oz/ 22 ml) French vermouth; stir well and serve.

ROYAL

Created for the opening of the Ritz Bar in Paris.
In a large wineglass: a dash (1/8 tsp/ .5 ml) of Angostura bitters on a small lump of sugar, a large piece of ice, a slice of lemon peel; fill with Ackerman-Laurance "Dry Royal" sparkling wine, stir, and serve.

ROYAL ROMANCE

In a shaker: one-fourth (1/2 oz/ 15 ml) each of passion fruit juice and Grand Marnier, half (1 oz/30 ml) gin; shake well and serve.

ROYAL SMILE

In a shaker: the juice of half a lime or a quarter lemon, a teaspoon (5 ml) of grenadine, half (1 oz/ 30 ml) gin, half (1 oz/30 ml) apple-jack (or calvados); shake well and serve.

RUSSIAN

In a shaker: a teaspoon (5 ml) each of crème de cacao and heavy cream, three-fourths (1 oz/45 ml) vodka; shake well and serve.

SARATOGA

In a shaker: crush one thin slice of ripe pineapple, a dash (1/8 tsp/.5 ml) each of orange bitters and maraschino, one glass (2 oz/60 ml) of brandy; shake well, strain into a fizz glass, fill with champagne, and serve.

SAZERAC

In a mixing glass: a dash (1/8 tsp/.5 ml) of Angostura bitters, a teaspoon (5 ml) of curaçao, one glass (2 oz/60 ml) of Sazerac brandy; stir well, pour into a chilled cocktail glass containing a dash (1/8 tsp/.5 ml) of pastis, and serve. There is often confusion between the "Sazerac" brandy cocktail and the "Zazarac" cocktail, originally made in New Orleans.

SENSATION

In a shaker: a teaspoon (5 ml) of maraschino, two or three sprigs of fresh mint, the juice of half a lime or a quarter lemon, half a glass (1 oz/30 ml) of Old Tom gin; shake well and serve.

SEVENTY-FIVE ("75")

In a shaker; a teaspoon (5 ml) of pastis, the juice of a quarter lemon, half a glass (1 oz/30 ml) of gin; shake well, strain into a small wineglass, fill with champagne, and serve.

SHAMROCK

In a mixing glass: one-fourth (1/2 oz/15 ml) each of green Chartreuse and French vermouth, half (1 oz/30 ml) Irish whiskey; stir well and serve.

SHANGHAI

In a shaker: a teaspoon (5 ml) of grenadine, a dash (1/8 tsp/.5 ml) of pastis, the juice of a quarter lemon, half a glass (1 oz/30 ml) of rum; shake well and serve.

SHERRY

In a mixing glass: two dashes (1/4 tsp/1 ml) of peach bitters, one glass (2 oz/60 ml) of sweet sherry; stir and serve.

SHROVE

In a mixing glass: a dash (⅛ tsp/ .5 ml) of pastis, half (1 oz/30 ml) French vermouth, half (1 oz/30 ml) sloe gin; stir well and serve.

SIDE CAR

In a shaker: one-fourth (½ oz/15 ml) each of lemon juice and curaçao triple sec, half (1 oz/30 ml) brandy; shake well and serve.

SILVER

In a mixing glass: a dash (⅛ tsp/.5 ml) each of orange bitters and maraschino, one-third (¾ oz/22 ml) French vermouth, two-thirds (1 ¼ oz/37 ml) gin; stir well and serve.

SILVER STREAK

In a shaker: half (1 oz/30 ml) kümmel, half (1 oz/30 ml) gin; shake well and serve. An after-dinner drink.

SLOE BERRY

In mixing glass: a dash (⅛ tsp/.5 ml) of Angostura bitters, one-third (¾ oz/22 ml) Italian vermouth, two-thirds (1 ¼ oz/37 ml) sloe gin; stir well and serve.

SODA

In a tumbler: a large piece of ice, a slice of lemon, half a teaspoon (2.5 ml) of sugar, a teaspoon (5 ml) of Angostura bitters, top with soda water; stir slightly and serve.

SOUTHERN CROSS

In a shaker: the juice of half a lime or a quarter lemon, half a tea-spoon (4 g) of sugar, a dash (⅛ tsp/.5 ml) of curaçao, half a glass (1 oz/30 ml) each of St. Croix rum and brandy; shake well, strain into a double cocktail glass, top with soda water, and serve.

S. S. MANHATTAN

In a shaker: a dash (⅛ tsp/.5 ml) of Bénédictine, half (1 oz/30 ml) orange juice, half (1 oz/30 ml) bourbon whiskey; shake well and serve.

S. S. WASHINGTON ◈

In a shaker: a dash (⅛ tsp/.5 ml) of grenadine, the juice of a quarter lemon, half (1 oz/30 ml) gin, half (1 oz/30 ml) rum; shake well and serve.

STAR

In a mixing glass: a dash (⅛ tsp/.5 ml) of orange bitters, one-third (¾ oz/22 ml) Italian vermouth, two-thirds (1 ¼ oz/37 ml) apple-jack (or calvados); stir and serve.

STINGER

In a shaker: one-third (¾ oz/22 ml) white crème de menthe, two-thirds (1 ¼ oz/37 ml) brandy; shake well and serve. An after-dinner drink.

SUISSESSE

In a shaker: half an egg white, the juice of half a lemon, one glass (2 oz/60 ml) of anisette; shake well, strain into a fizz glass, top with soda water, and serve.

SURE RELIEF

In a cocktail glass: a dash (⅛ tsp/.5 ml) of ginger ale, half (1 oz/30 ml) white crème de menthe, half (1 oz/30 ml) brandy; stir and serve.

TEMPTATION ◈

In a shaker: two-sixths (1 oz/30 ml) rum, one-sixth (½ oz/15 ml) lemon juice, half (1 ½ oz/45 ml) pastis; shake well and serve.

THIRD DEGREE

In a mixing glass: a teaspoon (5 ml) of pastis, one-third (¾ oz/22 ml) French vermouth, two-thirds (1 ¼ oz/37 ml) gin; stir well and serve.

TIN ROOF

This cocktail is usually "on the house," but the Ritz Bar has a tile roof!

T. N. T.

In a mixing glass: a dash (⅛ tsp/.5 ml) of Angostura bitters, half (1 oz/30 ml) Canadian whisky, half (1 oz/30 ml) pastis; stir well and serve.

TOM MOORE ◈

In a mixing glass: a dash (⅛ tsp/.5 ml) of Angostura bitters, one-third (¾ oz/22 ml) Italian ver-mouth, two-thirds (1 ¼ oz/37 ml) Irish whiskey; stir well and serve.

TOMATO JUICE*

In a shaker: crush one large ripe tomato, add celery salt to suit taste, half a teaspoon (2.5 ml) of Worcestershire sauce; shake well, strain into a double cocktail glass, and serve.

TOP SPEED ◈

In a shaker: one-fourth (1/2 oz/ 15 ml) pastis, one-fourth (1/2 oz/15 ml) French vermouth, half (1 oz/30 ml) brandy; shake well and serve.

TRINITY

In a mixing glass: one-third (1 oz/ 30 ml) each of gin, French vermouth, and Italian vermouth; stir well and serve.

TROPICAL

In a shaker: the juice of half a lime or a quarter lemon, a teaspoon (5 ml) of curaçao, half a glass (1 oz/30 ml) of rum; shake well and serve.

TUXEDO

In a mixing glass: a dash (1/8 tsp/ .5 ml) each of maraschino and pastis, half (1 oz/30 ml) French vermouth, half (1 oz/30 ml) gin; stir well and serve.

VALENCIA

In a shaker: the juice of a quarter orange, half a glass (1 oz/30 ml) of apricot brandy; shake well, strain into a fizz glass, fill with champagne, and serve.

WARD EIGHT

In a shaker: half a teaspoon (2.5 ml) of grenadine, one-third (1 oz/30 ml) each of lemon juice. rye whiskey, and gin; shake well and serve.

WHISKEY

In a mixing glass: a dash (1/8 tsp/ .5 ml) of Angostura bitters, a teaspoon (5 ml) of simple syrup, half a glass (1 oz/30 ml) of whiskey; stir well and serve with a maraschino cherry. Any whiskey may be used.

WHITE

In a mixing glass: a teaspoon (5 ml) of white curaçao, a dash (1/8 tsp/ .5 ml) of orange bitters, four-fifths (2 oz/60 ml) gin; stir well and serve.

*High-grade tomato juice is available in tins or bottles, is consistent in character, and is obtainable at very reasonable prices. It is advantageous to procure it in that form instead of from fresh tomatoes, which in most countries can be obtained only at particular seasons. Tomato juice in tins should, when opened, be removed to bottles or jugs, and in all cases should be kept on ice. The College Inn Food Product Co. of Chicago was the first to introduce this cocktail.

WHITE LADY

In a shaker: one-fourth (½ oz/ 15 ml) each of lemon juice and white curaçao, half (1 oz/30 ml) gin; shake well and serve.

WHITE ROSE

In a shaker: half an egg white, the juice of a quarter lemon, half a teaspoon (2 g) of sugar, one glass (2 oz) of gin; shake well, strain into a small wineglass, and serve.

WHITE SHADOW

In a shaker: one-third (1 oz/30 ml) each of heavy cream, pastis, and rye whiskey, a very small amount of grated nutmeg; shake well and serve.

WHIZ-BANG

In a mixing glass: a dash (⅛ tsp/ .5 ml) of pastis, a dash (⅛ tsp/ .5 ml) of grenadine, one glass (2 oz/60 ml) of Scotch whisky; stir well and serve.

WINTER SPORT ◈

In a shaker: a teaspoon (5 ml) of heavy cream, one-third (¾ oz/ 22 ml) gin, two-thirds (1 ¼ oz/ 37 ml) pastis; shake well and serve.

YALE

In a shaker: a dash (⅛ tsp/.5 ml) of Angostura bitters, one glass (2 oz/ 60 ml) of Old Tom gin; shake well, strain into a double cocktail glass, top with soda water, and serve.

YASHMAK

In a mixing glass: a dash (⅛ tsp/ .5 ml) of Angostura bitters, one-third (1 oz/30 ml) each of French vermouth, sweetened pastis, and rye whiskey; stir well and serve.

ZAZA

In a mixing glass: a dash (⅛ tsp/ .5 ml) of Angostura bitters, half (1 oz/30 ml) Dubonnet, half (1 oz/ 30 ml) gin; stir well and serve.

ZAZARAC

In a tumbler: dissolve a small lump of sugar in a little water, a dash (⅛ tsp/.5 ml) each of Angostura and orange bitters, a teaspoon (5 ml) of pastis, a piece of ice, one glass (2 oz/60 ml) of bourbon whiskey; add a lemon peel, top with soda water, stir well, and serve.

II.
MIXED
DRINKS

"A drunken poet emptied his glass in one go;
His companion warned him: 'Stop! You've had enough.'
Ready to sink from his chair, he replied: 'You are not wise,
One can drink too much, but one can never drink enough.'"

Gotthold Ephraim Lessing*

*German writer and playwright (1729–1781), famous notably for his *Fables*.

AFTER-DINNER DRINKS

BÉNÉDICTINE COCKTAIL

Rub the rim of a cocktail glass with a slice of lemon, dip the edge into powdered sugar, put in a maraschino cherry, and fill with the following mixture:

In a shaker: a dash (⅛ tsp/.5 ml) of Angostura bitters, one glass (2 oz/60 ml) of Bénédictine; shake slightly, strain into prepared glass, and serve.

**ANISETTE,
APRICOT BRANDY,
CHARTREUSE (yellow or green),
CHERRY BRANDY,
CORDIAL MEDOC,
CURAÇAO (red or white),
KÜMMEL,
MANDARINETTE,
MARASCHINO,
PEACH BRANDY,
PRUNELLE, etc.**

Same preparation as Bénédictine Cocktail with the liquor of your choice.

ICED APRICOT BRANDY

In a cocktail glass: three-fourths full of shaved ice; fill with apricot brandy and serve with straws.

**ANIS DELMONO,
ANISETTE,
BÉNÉDICTINE,
CHARTREUSE (yellow or green),
CHERRY BRANDY,
CORDIAL MEDOC,
CURAÇAO (red or white),
GRAND MARNIER,
KÜMMEL,
MANDARINETTE,
MARASCHINO,
MENTHE,
PEACH BRANDY,
VIELLE CURÉ, etc.**

Same preparation as Iced Apricot Brandy with the liquor of your choice.

COBBLERS

BRANDY COBBLER

In a tumbler three-fourths full of cracked ice: half a teaspoon (4 g) of sugar, a teaspoon (5 ml) of curaçao, one glass (2 oz/60 ml) of brandy; stir, decorate with seasonal fruit, and serve with a spoon.

CHAMPAGNE COBBLER

In a tumbler two-thirds full of cracked ice: a teaspoon (5 ml) each of lemon juice and curaçao; fill with champagne, stir, add a slice of orange or pineapple, and serve with straws.

CLARET COBBLER*

In a tumbler half filled with cracked ice: a dash (1/8 tsp/.5 ml) of maraschino, a teaspoon each of sugar (5 g) and lemon juice (5 ml); fill with claret, stir, decorate with seasonal fruit, and serve with a spoon.

PORT COBBLER

In a tumbler two-thirds full of cracked ice: a teaspoon (5 ml) each of orange juice and curaçao, very little or no sugar, fill with port, decorate with seasonal fruit, and serve with a spoon.

RHINE WINE COBBLER

In a tumbler half filled with cracked ice: a teaspoon (5 ml) each of sugar and lemon juice; fill with Rhine wine, stir slightly, decorate with seasonal fruit, and serve with a spoon.

*The claret referred to here is a light red wine, very lightly colored, "easy to drink," and low in tannins, shipped to England from Bordeaux and highly prized by the English in the Middle Ages. The word "claret" is still used in English to refer to the best red Bordeaux wines.

RUM or WHISKEY COBBLER

Same preparation as Brandy Cobbler with the liquor of your choice.

SAUTERNES COBBLER

In a tumbler half filled with cracked ice: a teaspoon (5 ml) of lemon juice; fill with Sauternes wine, stir slightly, decorate with seasonal fruit, and serve with a spoon.

SHERRY COBBLER

In a tumbler two-thirds full of cracked ice: a teaspoon (5 ml) each of sugar and orange juice; fill with sweet sherry, stir slightly, decorate with seasonal fruit, and serve with a spoon.

BRANDY, RUM, or WHISKEY COLLINS

Same preparation as John (or Tom) Collins with the liquor of your choice.

JOHN or TOM COLLINS

In a large tumbler: two or three pieces of ice, the juice of half a lemon, a teaspoon (4 g) of sugar, one glass (2 oz/60 ml) of gin; top with soda water, stir well, and serve.

COOLERS

APRICOT BRANDY COOLER

In a large tumbler: two or three pieces of ice, a dash (⅛ tsp/.5 ml) of Angostura bitters, the juice of half a lemon, a teaspoon (5 ml) of grenadine, one glass (2 oz/60 ml) of apricot brandy; stir slightly while topping with soda water and serve.

BRANDY or RUM COOLER

Same preparation as Apricot Brandy Cooler with the liquor of your choice.

HAWAIIAN COOLER

In a large tumbler: two pieces of ice in whole orange rind, one glass (2 oz/60 ml) of rye whiskey; top with soda water, stir slightly, and serve.

IRISH WHISKEY COOLER

In a large tumbler: two pieces of ice in whole lemon rind, one glass (2 oz/60 ml) of Irish whiskey; top with soda water, stir slightly, and serve.

REMSEN COOLER

In a large tumbler: two pieces of ice in whole lemon rind, one glass (2 oz/60 ml) of Old Tom gin; top with soda water, stir slightly, and serve.

SARATOGA COOLER

In a large tumbler: three or four pieces of ice, the juice of one lime, half a teaspoon (2 g) of sugar; top with ginger ale, stir slightly, and serve.

SCOTCH WHISKY COOLER

In a large tumbler: two pieces of ice in whole lemon rind, one glass (2 oz/60 ml) of Scotch whisky; top with soda water, stir slightly, and serve.

ZENITH COOLER

In a large tumbler: three or four pieces of ice, a tablespoon (15 ml) of pineapple syrup, one glass (2 oz/60 ml) of gin; stir slightly while topping with soda water and serve with a slice of pineapple.

BRANDY CRUSTA

Rub the rim of a wineglass with a slice of lemon, dip the edge in powdered sugar, then fit the rind of half an orange into the bottom of the glass, add in a maraschino cherry, and fill with the following mixture prepared in a shaker: a dash (⅛ tsp/.5 ml) of Angostura bitters, one teaspoon (5 ml) each of lemon juice and maraschino, one glass (2 oz/60 ml) of brandy; shake well, strain into prepared glass, and serve.

GIN, RUM, or WHISKEY CRUSTA

Same preparation as Brandy Crusta with the liquor of your choice.

CUPS

A FEW SPRIGS OF FRESH MINT MAY BE ADDED IN MOST CUPS, EXCEPT THE CIDER AND THE VELVET CUP.

CHABLIS or POUILLY CUP

FOR SIX DRINKS

In a half-gallon pitcher (about 2 L): a large piece of ice, one glass (2 oz/ 60 ml) of Bénédictine, three thin slices of ripe pineapple, one bottle of Chablis, Pouilly, or other white Burgundy wine; stir gently and serve. The pineapple can be replaced with two peeled ripe peaches.

CIDER CUP

FOR TEN DRINKS

In a half-gallon pitcher (about 2 L): a large piece of ice, one peeled orange in slices, one glass (2 oz/60 ml) each of applejack (or calvados), maraschino, and curaçao, one quart (1 L) of sweet cider, top with soda water; stir gently, add seasonal fruit, and serve.

CLARET or BURGUNDY CUP

FOR SIX DRINKS

In a half-gallon pitcher (about 2 L): a large piece of ice, three thin slices of ripe pineapple crushed with their juice retained, one glass (2 oz/60 ml) of maraschino, a tablespoon (8 g) of powdered sugar, one quart (1 L) of claret or red Burgundy wine; stir gently and serve.

GINGER ALE CUP
FOR SIX DRINKS
In a half-gallon pitcher (about 2 L): a large piece of ice, one peeled lemon in slices, the juice of one orange, two glasses (4 oz/120 ml) of brandy, one glass (2 oz / 60 ml) of maraschino, three pints (1.7 L) of ginger ale; stir until very cold and serve.

GRAPEFRUIT CUP
FOR TWELVE DRINKS
In a gallon pitcher or bowl (about 4 L): a large piece of ice, a bottle of brandy, one glass (2 oz/60 ml) of grenadine, three grapefruits with rinds and membranes removed, a one-pound can (about 450 ml) of sweetened grapefruit juice, half a bottle of soda water; stir well and serve.

KALTE ENTE
FOR TEN DRINKS
In a half-gallon pitcher (about 2 L) with a whole lemon rind rested over the brim, add one glass (2 oz/ 60 ml) of curaçao, one quart (1 L) of thoroughly chilled Moselle wine, and one quart (1 L) of thoroughly chilled sparkling Rhine wine. No need to stir before serving.

MAI WEIN CUP*
FOR TWENTY DRINKS
In a gallon pitcher (about 4 L) with a large piece of ice, soak a big bunch of young woodruff** in three quarts (3 L) of light Moselle wine for one hour, six lumps of sugar (2 tbsp/25 g), one glass (2 oz/60 ml) each of curaçao and brandy, add one (1 L) of sparkling Moselle when ready to serve.

MOSELLE CUP
FOR TWELVE DRINKS
In a gallon pitcher (about 4 L): a large piece of ice, three ripe peeled peaches cut into quarters, a dozen maraschino cherries, one glass (2 oz/60 ml) of Bénédictine, one bottle of still Moselle wine, one bottle of sparkling Moselle wine; stir gently and serve. Powdered sugar may be added to suit taste.

PEACH CUP
FOR SIX DRINKS
In a half-gallon pitcher (about 2 L): a large piece of ice, two ripe whole peaches pierced with a fork, one quart (1 L) of light Rhine wine; stir gently and serve. Powdered sugar may be added to suit taste.

*"May wine" in German.
**In Germany and the regions surrounding the Rhine, this plant is very commonly used to flavor liqueurs.

RHINE WINE CUP

FOR SIX DRINKS

In a half-gallon pitcher (about 2 L): a large piece of ice, one peeled orange in slices, one glass (2 oz/60 ml) of curaçao, one bottle of Rhine wine, top with soda water; stir gently and serve. Powdered sugar may be added to suit taste.

SAUTERNES CUP n° 1

FOR SIX DRINKS

In a half-gallon pitcher (about 2 L): squeeze half a pound of currants (225 g), retaining the juice, a large piece of ice, one bottle of Sauternes wine; stir gently and serve.

SAUTERNES CUP n° 2

FOR TEN DRINKS

In a half-gallon pitcher (about 2 L): a large piece of ice, one peeled lemon cut into slices, one glass (2 oz/60 ml) of curaçao, one glass (2 oz/60 ml) of brandy, a dozen maraschino cherries, one bottle of Sauternes wine; top with soda water, a long slice of cucumber rind, stir gently, and serve.

SPARKLING RHINE WINE CUP

FOR TEN DRINKS

In a gallon pitcher (about 4 L): a large piece of ice, a long slice of cucumber rind, two ripe pears peeled, quartered, and cored; one glass (2 oz/60 ml) each of maraschino, curaçao, and brandy, a bottle of sparkling Rhine wine; top with soda water, stir gently, and serve.

VELVET CUP

FOR TEN DRINKS

In a half-gallon pitcher (about 2 L) with a large piece of ice, pour gently (to avoid overflowing) one quart (1 L) of stout and one quart (1 L) of sweet champagne; stir very gently and serve.

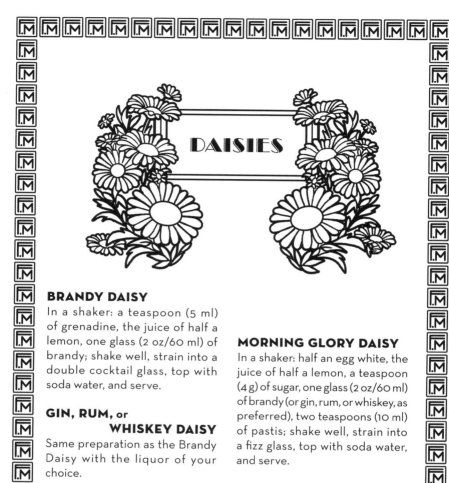

DAISIES

BRANDY DAISY

In a shaker: a teaspoon (5 ml) of grenadine, the juice of half a lemon, one glass (2 oz/60 ml) of brandy; shake well, strain into a double cocktail glass, top with soda water, and serve.

GIN, RUM, or
WHISKEY DAISY

Same preparation as the Brandy Daisy with the liquor of your choice.

MORNING GLORY DAISY

In a shaker: half an egg white, the juice of half a lemon, a teaspoon (4 g) of sugar, one glass (2 oz/60 ml) of brandy (or gin, rum, or whiskey, as preferred), two teaspoons (10 ml) of pastis; shake well, strain into a fizz glass, top with soda water, and serve.

STAR DAISY

Same preparation as Brandy Daisy, except with applejack (or calvados).

EGG NOGS*

BALTIMORE EGG NOG

In a shaker: one fresh egg, a teaspoon (4 g) of sugar, half a glass (1 oz/30 ml) each of Madeira wine and bourbon whiskey, one glass (2 oz/60 ml) of milk; shake well, strain into a tumbler, serve with grated nutmeg.

EGG NOG

In a shaker: one fresh egg, a teaspoon (4 g) of sugar, half a glass (1 oz/30 ml) each of brandy and rum, one glass (1 oz/30 ml) of milk; shake well, strain into a tumbler, and serve with grated nutmeg if desired.

EGG NOG—HOT

In a heated tumbler: a teaspoon (4 g) of sugar, one egg yolk, half a glass (1 oz/30 ml) each of rum and brandy; stir until ingredients are well mixed, add boiling milk to fill tumbler while stirring, and serve with grated nutmeg if desired.

*Egg Nogs (hot or cold) may be made with brandy, gin, rum, sherry, or whiskey.

FIXES

BRANDY FIX

In a small tumbler: the juice of half a lemon, a teaspoon (4 g) of sugar, a dash (⅛ tsp/.5 ml) of curaçao, one glass (2 oz/60 ml) of brandy; fill with shaved ice, stir, decorate with a slice of orange and seasonal berries, and serve with straws.

GIN, RUM, or WHISKEY FIX

Same preparation as Brandy Fix with the liquor of your choice.

FIZZES

AMERICAN FIZZ

In a shaker: the juice of half a lemon, half a glass (1 oz/30 ml) each of brandy and gin, a teaspoon (5 ml) of grenadine; shake well, strain into a fizz glass, top with soda water, and serve.

BACARDI FIZZ

In a shaker: the juice of half a lemon, a teaspoon (4 g) of sugar, one glass (2 oz/60 ml) of Bacardi rum; shake well, strain into a fizz glass, top with soda water, and serve.

BISMARCK FIZZ or SLOE GIN FIZZ

In a shaker: the juice of half a lemon, one glass (2 oz/60 ml) of sloe gin; shake well, strain into a fizz glass, top with soda water, and serve.

BRANDY FIZZ

In a shaker: the juice of half a lemon, a teaspoon (4 g) of sugar, one glass (2 oz/60 ml) of brandy; shake well, strain into a fizz glass, top with soda water, and serve.

BUCK'S FIZZ

In a shaker: the juice of half an orange, half a teaspoon (2 g) of sugar, half a glass (1 oz/30 ml) of gin; shake well, strain into a fizz glass, fill with champagne, and serve.

DIAMOND FIZZ

In a shaker: the juice of half a lemon, half a teaspoon (2 g) of sugar, half a glass (1 oz/30 ml) of gin; shake well, strain into a fizz glass, fill with champagne, and serve.

DUBONNET FIZZ

In a shaker: the juice of half an orange, one glass (2 oz/60 ml) of Dubonnet; shake slightly, strain into a fizz glass, fill with champagne, and serve.

FRANK'S SPECIAL GIN FIZZ

In a shaker: the juice of half a lemon, half a teaspoon (4 g) of sugar, a quarter of crushed peach, one glass (2 oz/60 ml) of gin; shake well, strain into a tumbler, top with soda water, and serve.

GIN FIZZ

In a shaker: the juice of half a lemon, a teaspoon (4 g) of sugar, one glass (2 oz/60 ml) of gin; shake well, strain into a fizz glass, top with soda water, and serve.

GOLDEN FIZZ

In a shaker: the juice of half a lemon, a teaspoon (4 g) of sugar, one egg yolk, one glass (2 oz/60 ml) of gin; shake well, strain into a tumbler, top with soda water, and serve.

GRENADINE GIN FIZZ

In a shaker: the juice of half a lemon, two teaspoons (10 ml) of grenadine, one glass (2 oz/60 ml) of gin; shake well, strain into a fizz glass, top with soda water, and serve.

HOFFMAN HOUSE or CREAM GIN FIZZ

In a shaker: the juice of half a lemon, a teaspoon each of sugar (4 g) and heavy cream (5 ml), one glass (2 oz/60 ml) of gin; shake well, strain into a tumbler, top with soda water, and serve.

HOLLAND GIN FIZZ

In a shaker: the juice of half a lemon, a teaspoon (4 g) of sugar, one glass (2 oz/60 ml) of Holland gin; shake well, strain into a fizz glass, top with soda water, and serve.

IMPERIAL FIZZ

In a shaker: the juice of half a lemon, a teaspoon (4 g) of sugar, half a glass (1 oz/30 ml) of rye or bourbon whiskey; shake well, strain into a fizz glass, fill with champagne, and serve.

IRISH WHISKEY FIZZ

In a shaker: the juice of half a lemon, half a teaspoon (4 g) of sugar, a teaspoon (5 ml) of curaçao, one glass (2 oz/60 ml) of Irish whiskey; shake well, strain into a fizz glass, top with soda water, and serve.

JUBILEE FIZZ ◈

In a shaker: half a glass (1 oz/30 ml) of unsweetened pineapple juice, half a glass (1 oz/30 ml) of gin; shake well, strain into a fizz glass, fill with champagne, and serve.

MORNING GLORY FIZZ

In a shaker: the juice of half a lemon, a teaspoon (4 g) of sugar, half an egg white, two dashes of pastis, one glass (1 oz/30 ml) of Scotch whisky; shake well, strain into a tumbler, top with soda water, and serve.

NEW ORLEANS FIZZ

In a shaker: half an egg white, the juice of half a lemon, a teaspoon each of sugar (4 g) and heavy cream (5 ml), a dash (⅛ tsp/.5 ml) of orange blossom water, one glass (2 oz/60 ml) of gin; shake well, strain into a tumbler, top with soda water, and serve.

NICKY'S FIZZ ◈

Special for Prince Nicolas Toumanoff.

In a shaker: half a glass (1 oz/30 ml) of sweetened grapefruit juice, one glass (2 oz/60 ml) of gin; shake well, strain into a fizz glass, top with soda water, and serve.

ORANGE FIZZ

In a shaker: the juice of half an orange, a dash (⅛ tsp/.5 ml) of grenadine, one glass (2 oz/60 ml) of gin; shake well, strain into a fizz glass, top with soda water, and serve.

PINEAPPLE FIZZ

In a shaker: half a glass (1 oz/30 ml) of sweetened pineapple juice, one glass (2 oz/60 ml) of gin; shake well, strain into a fizz glass, top with soda water, and serve.

ROYAL GIN FIZZ

In a shaker: the juice of half a lemon, a teaspoon (4 g) of sugar, one fresh egg, half a glass (1 oz/30 ml) of gin; shake well, strain into a tumbler, top with soda water, and serve.

RUBY FIZZ

In a shaker: the juice of half a lemon, a teaspoon (5 ml) of raspberry syrup, half an egg white, one glass (2 oz/60 ml) of sloe gin; shake well, strain into a tumbler, top with soda water, and serve.

RUM FIZZ

In a shaker: the juice of half a lemon, half a teaspoon (4 g) of sugar, a teaspoon (5 ml) of cherry brandy, half a glass (1 oz/30 ml) of rum; shake well, strain into a fizz glass, top with soda water, and serve.

SCOTCH WHISKY FIZZ

In a shaker: the juice of half a lemon, a teaspoon (4 g) of sugar, one glass (2 oz/60 ml) of Scotch whisky; shake well, strain into a fizz glass, top with soda water, and serve.

SEAPEA "C.P." ◈

Special for Mr. Cole Porter, famous composer of lyrics and music.
In a shaker: the juice of half a lemon, one glass (2 oz/60 ml) of sweetened pastis; shake well, strain into a fizz glass, top with soda water, and serve.

SILVER FIZZ

In a shaker: the juice of half a lemon, a teaspoon (4 g) of sugar, half an egg white, one glass (2 oz/60 ml) of gin; shake well, strain into a tumbler, top with soda water, and serve.

SOUR GIN FIZZ

In a shaker: the juice of half a lemon, one glass (2 oz/60 ml) of Old Tom gin; shake well, strain into a fizz glass, top with soda water, and serve.

SOUTHSIDE FIZZ

In a shaker: the juice of half a lemon, a teaspoon (4 g) of sugar, three sprigs of mint, half a glass (1 oz/30 ml) of gin; shake well, strain into a fizz glass, top with soda water, and serve.

STRAWBERRY FIZZ

In a shaker: the juice of half a lemon, half a teaspoon (2 g) of sugar, three or four crushed strawberries, half a glass (1 oz/30 ml) of gin; shake well, strain into a fizz glass, top with soda water, and serve.

TEXAS FIZZ

In a shaker: the juices of a quarter lemon and a quarter orange, a dash (1/8 tsp/.5 ml) of grenadine, half a glass (1 oz/30 ml) of gin; shake well, strain into a fizz glass, fill with champagne, and serve.

VIOLET FIZZ

In a shaker: the juice of half a lemon, a teaspoon (5 ml) each of raspberry syrup and heavy cream, half a glass (1 oz/30 ml) of gin; shake well, strain into a fizz glass, top with soda water, and serve.

FLIPS

ALE FLIP

In a tumbler: half a teaspoon (2 g) of sugar, one egg yolk mixed thoroughly with a little ale; fill glass with cold ale while stirring gently and serve. May be served hot by heating the ale.

BOSTON FLIP

In a shaker: one fresh egg, a teaspoon (4 g) of sugar, half a glass (1 oz/30 ml) each of Madeira and rye whiskey; shake well, strain into a double cocktail glass, and serve with grated nutmeg.

BRANDY or EGG FLIP

In a shaker: one fresh egg, a teaspoon (4 g) of sugar, one glass (2 oz/60 ml) of brandy; shake well, strain into a double cocktail glass, and serve with grated nutmeg.

GIN, RUM, or WHISKEY FLIP

Same preparation as the Brandy Flip with the liquor of your choice.

LEMON FLIP

In a shaker: one fresh egg, a teaspoon (4 g) of sugar, the juice of one lemon: shake well, strain into a small wineglass, and serve.

PORT FLIP

In a shaker: one fresh egg, half a teaspoon (2 g) of sugar (optional), one glass (2 oz/60 ml) of port; shake well, strain into a double cocktail glass, and serve with grated nutmeg if desired.

SHERRY FLIP

In a shaker: one fresh egg, half a teaspoon (2 g) of sugar, one glass (2 oz/60 ml) of sherry; shake well, strain into a double cocktail glass, and serve with grated nutmeg if desired.

BRANDY HIGHBALL

In a tumbler: a large piece of ice, one glass (2 oz/60 ml) of brandy; top with soda water and serve.

GIN, PEACH BRANDY, RUM, or WHISKEY HIGHBALL

Same preparation as Brandy Highball with the liquor of your choice.

CHAMPAGNE JULEP

In a large tumbler: crush four sprigs of mint with one lump of sugar in a little water, then half fill with cracked ice and add one glass (2 oz/60 ml) of brandy; pour in champagne, stir slowly, decorate with a slice of pineapple or orange, and serve with straws.

MINT JULEP

In a large tumbler half filled with shaved ice: a teaspoon (4 g) of sugar, five or six sprigs of mint, one glass (2 oz/60 ml) of bourbon whiskey; stir vigorously to bruise the mint and mix with the whiskey; add more shaved ice and stir until glass is thoroughly frosted; decorate with a sprig of mint and a slice of lemon, and serve with straws.

PINEAPPLE JULEP
FOR TWENTY-FIVE DRINKS

In a very large bowl or container: a big chunk of ice, the juice of two oranges, one glass (2 oz/60 ml) each of raspberry syrup and maraschino, two glasses (4 oz/120 ml) of gin, two quarts (2 L) of Ackerman-Laurance "Dry Royal" sparkling Saumur wine, one ripe pineapple peeled and crushed, one pound (450 g) of fresh berries; stir mixture until cold and serve in a wineglass with a spoon. Just before serving, add a tablespoon (12 g) of sugar to produce effervescence.

RUM, BRANDY, GIN, or WHISKEY JULEP

Same preparation as Mint Julep with the liquor of your choice.

*In 1767, the chemist Joseph Priestly invented the first soda with a carbonated water base, which he called a "julep."

79

LEMONADES

ANGOSTURA LEMONADE
Plain lemonade with a teaspoon (5 ml) of Angostura bitters.

BRANDY, CLARET, RUM, or WHISKEY LEMONADE
Same recipe as plain lemonade with the liquor of your choice.

EGG LEMONADE
In a shaker: the juice of half a lemon, a teaspoon (4 g) of sugar, one fresh egg; shake well, pour into a tumbler, top with plain water or soda water, and serve.

FRUIT LEMONADE
Plain lemonade with a slice of pineapple and seasonal fruit; serve with a spoon.

LEMON SQUASH
Same recipe as plain lemonade with soda water instead of plain water.

LEMONADE (Plain)
In a tumbler: two or three pieces of ice, the juice of one lemon, a teaspoon (4 g) of sugar; fill with plain water, stir, and serve.

ORANGEADE
In a tumbler: two or three pieces of ice, the juice of one orange, a teaspoon (5 ml) of grenadine; top with plain water, stir, and serve.

ORGEAT LEMONADE
In a tumbler: two or three pieces of ice, the juice of half a lemon, one glass (2 oz/60 ml) of almond syrup; top with soda water, stir, and serve.

RASPBERRY LEMONADE

In a tumbler: two or three pieces of ice, the juice of one lemon, a tablespoon (15 ml) of raspberry syrup; top with soda water, stir, and serve.

STRAWBERRY LEMONADE

In a tumbler: two or three pieces of ice, the juice of one lemon, a tablespoon (15 ml) of strawberry syrup; top with soda water, stir, and serve.

PUFFS

BRANDY PUFF

In a tumbler: a piece of ice, one glass (2 oz/60 ml) of brandy, one glass (2 oz) of fresh milk; top with soda water, stir slightly, and serve.

GIN, RUM, or WHISKEY PUFF

Same preparation as Brandy Puff with the liquor of your choice.

PUNCHES

FOR ENTERTAINING AT HOME

FRANK'S SPECIAL PUNCH
FOR ABOUT FIFTY DRINKS

In a large bowl or tureen, taking care to not waste the fruit juices: two pounds (900 g) of ripe pineapple cut into cubes and crushed, one pound (450 g) of ripe cherries with stones removed, six peeled grapefruits with seeds and cells removed, one pound (450 g) of powdered sugar, half a bottle of Bénédictine, one bottle of brandy; mix well and put into the refrigerator until very cold. When ready to serve, pour two tablespoons (30 ml) of the mixture (fruits, juices, and liquors) into a large wineglass, fill with thoroughly chilled dry champagne, and serve with a spoon.

Second possible fruit combination:

Two pounds (900 g) of ripe strawberries, twelve sliced bananas, and twelve peeled and sliced peaches.

Third possible fruit combination:

Twelve peeled oranges with seeds and cells removed, ten to twelve peeled, sliced, and cored pears, and one pint (300 g) of maraschino cherries.

Do not mix hard and soft fruits in either fruit combination.

APRICOT or PEACH BRANDY, GIN, RUM, or WHISKEY PUNCH

Same preparation as Brandy Punch with the liquor of your choice.

BRANDY PUNCH

In a tumbler: half a teaspoon (2 g) of sugar dissolved in a little water, a teaspoon (5 ml) of raspberry syrup, the juice of half a lemon, one glass (2 oz/60 ml) of brandy; fill with shaved ice, stir well, decorate with seasonal berries and an orange slice, and serve with a spoon and straws.

CHAMPAGNE PUNCH

In a tumbler half filled with cracked ice: the juice of half a lemon, half a glass (1 oz/30 ml) of strawberry or raspberry syrup; fill with champagne, stir slightly, add an orange slice, and serve with straws.

CHRISTMAS PUNCH
FOR ABOUT FIFTY DRINKS

In a three-gallon tureen or other container: a quart (1 L) of strong tea, a bottle each of rum, rye whiskey, and brandy, half a bottle of Bénédictine, a tablespoon (15 ml) of Angostura bitters; peel and grate into mixture a two- or three-pound (1-1.5 kg) ripe pineapple. Add the juice of twelve oranges, one pound or more (450 g) of pre-dissolved sugar in ample water; mix well and put into the refrigerator until very cold. Have two quarts (2 L) of thoroughly chilled champagne ready to add and serve in a wineglass with a spoon.

CHRISTMAS PUNCH— HOT
FOR TWENTY DRINKS

In a saucepan or tureen measuring one gallon or larger: two bottles of brandy, two bottles of champagne, one pound (450 g) of sugar, one pound (450 g) of ripe pineapple cut in cubes and crushed; heat to a simmer, but do not boil, then pour a little brandy on top, set aflame, allow to burn one minute, and serve in a heated wineglass with a spoon.

CLARET or BURGUNDY PUNCH n° 1

In a tumbler half filled with cracked ice: a teaspoon each of lemon juice (5 ml), sugar (4 g), and maraschino (5 ml); fill with claret or red Burgundy wine, stir, add an orange slice and seasonal fruit, and serve with a spoon.

CLARET or BURGUNDY PUNCH n° 2

In a tumbler half filled with cracked ice: a teaspoon (5 ml) each of lemon juice, grenadine, and curaçao; fill with claret or red Burgundy wine, stir, add an orange slice, and serve with straws.

CURAÇAO PUNCH

In a tumbler: half a teaspoon (2 g) of sugar, the juice of half a lemon, half a glass (1 oz/30 ml) of curaçao, half a glass (1 oz/30 ml) of brandy or rum; fill with shaved ice, stir slightly, decorate with a small slice of pineapple and seasonal berries, and serve with a spoon and straws.

FISH HOUSE PUNCH

In a tumbler: two or three pieces of ice, the juice of half a lemon, a teaspoon (4 g) of sugar, half a glass (1 oz/30 ml) each of rum, brandy, Bénédictine, and peach brandy; top with soda water, stir, and serve.

MILK PUNCH

In a shaker: a teaspoon (4 g) of sugar, half a glass (1 oz/30 ml) each of brandy and rum, one glass (2 oz/60 ml) of milk; shake, allow foam to settle, strain into a tumbler, grate nutmeg on top, and serve.

PISCO PUNCH

In a large wineglass: a piece of ice, a teaspoon (5 ml) each of pineapple and lemon juice, one glass (2 oz/60 ml) of pisco; add plain water, a small slice of pineapple, stir, and serve.

PLANTER'S PUNCH

In a tumbler: two or three pieces of ice, a dash (1/8 tsp/.5 ml) of Angostura bitters, the juice of half a lime or a quarter lemon, a teaspoon (5 ml) of grenadine, and one glass (2 oz/60 ml) of rum; top with soda water, stir, and serve.

ROMAN PUNCH

In a tumbler: the juice of half a lemon, half a glass (1 oz/30 ml) each of raspberry syrup, rum, and brandy; fill with shaved ice, stir well, add seasonal berries, a dash (1/8 tsp/.5 ml) of port, and serve with a spoon and straws.

SAUTERNES PUNCH

In a tumbler half filled with cracked ice: half a teaspoon (2 g) of sugar, the juice of half a lemon, a teaspoon (5 ml) of curaçao; fill with Sauternes wine, stir well, decorate with seasonal fruit, and serve with a spoon and straws.

STRAWBERRY PUNCH

In a tumbler: half a teaspoon (2 g) of sugar dissolved in a little water, the juice of half a lemon, a teaspoon (5 ml) of strawberry syrup, one glass (2 oz/60 ml) of brandy; fill with shaved ice, stir, add strawberries, and serve with a spoon and straws.

SWEDISH PUNCH—HOT

In a small heated tumbler: one glass (2 oz/60 ml) of caloric punsch*; fill with boiling water and serve with a slice of lemon.

*Swedish liqueur.

RICKEYS

APRICOT BRANDY, BRANDY, RUM, SLOE GIN, or WHISKEY RICKEY

Same preparation as Gin Rickey with the liquor of your choice.

GIN RICKEY

In a small tumbler: a piece of ice, the juice of half a lime squeezed directly into the tumbler, one glass (2 oz/60 ml) of gin; top with soda water, stir slightly, and serve. (The juice of a quarter lemon may be used instead of the lime.)

SANGAREES

ALE, PORTER, or STOUT SANGAREE

In a large tumbler: half a teaspoon (2 g) of sugar dissolved in a little water; fill with cold ale, porter, or stout, stir slightly, grate nutmeg on top, and serve.

BRANDY SANGAREE

In a small tumbler: half a teaspoon (2 g) of sugar dissolved in a little water, a piece of ice, one glass (2 oz/60 ml) of brandy; stir, grate nutmeg on top, and serve.

GIN, PORT, RUM, SHERRY, or WHISKEY SANGAREE

Same preparation as Brandy Sangaree with the liquor of your choice.

BRANDY SCAFFA

In cocktail glass: a dash (⅛ tsp/ .5 ml) of Angostura bitters, half (1 oz/30 ml) maraschino, half (1 oz/ 30 ml) brandy; stir and serve.

GIN SCAFFA

In a cocktail glass: a dash (⅛ tsp/ .5 ml) of Angostura bitters, half (1 oz/30 ml) Bénédictine, half (1 oz/30 ml) gin; stir and serve.

RUM SCAFFA

In a cocktail glass: a dash (⅛ tsp/ .5 ml) of Angostura bitters, half (1 oz/30 ml) Bénédictine, half (1 oz/ 30 ml) rum; stir and serve.

WHISKEY SCAFFA

In a cocktail glass: a dash (⅛ tsp/ .5 ml) of Angostura bitters, half (1 oz/30 ml) Bénédictine, half (1 oz/30 ml) bourbon or other whiskey; stir and serve.

SHRUBS ARE MADE OF BRANDY, RUM, SHERRY, LEMONS, ORANGES, AND COOKED FRUIT SUCH AS CURRANTS, CHERRIES, AND RASPBERRIES. THEY SHOULD BE SERVED HOT LIKE GROGS. THEY CAN ALSO BE PREPARED COLD AND ARE DELIGHTFUL SUMMER DRINKS.

BRANDY SHRUB

In a two-gallon (about 7.5 L) pitcher or larger container: one gallon (3.8 L) of brandy, the rinds of three lemons, the juice of twelve lemons, cover and let sit for forty-eight hours, then add two quarts (2 L) of sweet sherry, two pounds (900 g) of sugar dissolved in a little water; mix well, strain through cheesecloth, and bottle.

BRANDY or RUM SHRUB—COLD

In a tumbler: a piece of ice, one glass (2 oz/60 ml) of shrub, top with plain water or soda water, and serve.

RUM SHRUB

In a three-gallon (about 11 L) pitcher or other container: one gallon (3.8 L) of rum, the juice of about ten pounds (4.5 kg) of cooked currants, two pounds (900 g) of sugar dissolved in a little water; cover and let sit for one week or more, mix well, strain through cheesecloth, and bottle.

SLINGS

GIN, RUM, or WHISKEY SLING

Same preparation as Brandy Sling with the liquor of your choice.

BRANDY SLING

In a tumbler: three or four pieces of ice, a dash (1/8 tsp/.5 ml) of Angostura bitters, the juice of half a lemon, a teaspoon (4 g) of sugar, one glass (2 oz/60 ml) of brandy; fill with plain water, shake well, and serve.

SINGAPORE SLING

In a tumbler: three or four pieces of ice, the juice of half a lemon, half a glass (1 oz/30 ml) of cherry brandy, half a glass (1 oz/30 ml) of gin; fill with plain water, shake well, and serve.

SMASHES

BRANDY SMASH

"Actually a miniature Julep." In a small tumbler: dissolve half a teaspoon (2 g) of sugar in a little water, add two or three sprigs of mint, one glass (2 oz/60 ml) of brandy; fill with shaved ice, stir until very cold, add a slice of lemon, and serve with straws.

GIN, RUM, or WHISKEY SMASH

Same preparation as Brandy Smash with the liquor of your choice.

APPLEJACK (OR CALVADOS), GIN, RUM, or WHISKEY SOUR

Same preparation as Brandy Sour with the liquor of your choice.

BRANDY SOUR

In a shaker: the juice of half a lemon, half a teaspoon (2 g) of sugar, one glass (2 oz/60 ml) of brandy; shake well, strain into a double cocktail glass, top with soda water, and serve.

APPLEJACK or
CALVADOS TODDY

In a small tumbler: a teaspoon of sugar (4 g) dissolved in a little water, leaving the spoon in the tumbler, a piece of ice, one glass (2 oz/60 ml) of applejack (or calvados); stir and serve with a glass of water.

BRANDY, GIN, PEACH
BRANDY, RUM, or
WHISKEY TODDY

Same preparation as Applejack Toddy with the liquor of your choice.

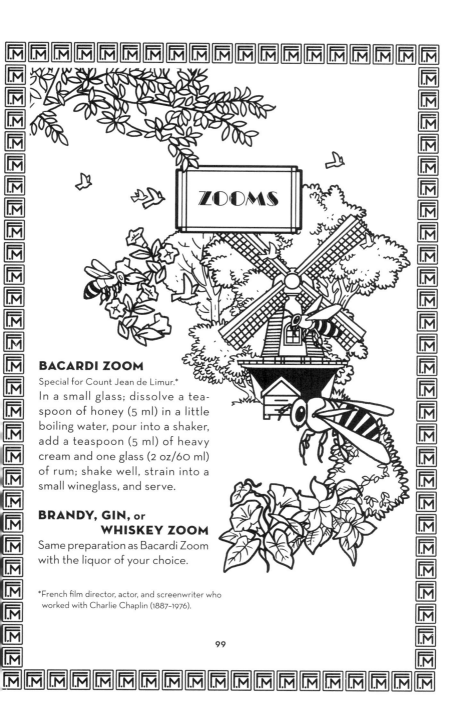

ZOOMS

BACARDI ZOOM

Special for Count Jean de Limur.*
In a small glass; dissolve a teaspoon of honey (5 ml) in a little
boiling water, pour into a shaker,
add a teaspoon (5 ml) of heavy
cream and one glass (2 oz/60 ml)
of rum; shake well, strain into a
small wineglass, and serve.

BRANDY, GIN, or WHISKEY ZOOM

Same preparation as Bacardi Zoom
with the liquor of your choice.

*French film director, actor, and screenwriter who
worked with Charlie Chaplin (1887–1976).

HOT DRINKS

AMERICAN GROG

In a heated tumbler: one glass (2 oz/ 60 ml) of rum, a slice of lemon; add boiling water to suit taste and serve.

APPLEJACK or
CALVADOS GROG

In a small heated tumbler: dissolve a teaspoon (4 g or more) of sugar in a little boiling water, leave the spoon in the glass, add a quarter of a small baked apple, a glass (2 oz/60 ml) of applejack (or calvados); pour in boiling water according to the desired taste and serve.

BLACK STRIPE

In a small, heated tumbler: a tea- spoon (5 ml) of molasses, one glass (2 oz/60 ml) of rum; add boiling water to suit taste, stir, and serve.

BLUE BLAZER

Heat two large cups: in one cup, a teaspoon (4 g) of sugar dissolved in boiling water; in the other cup, one glass (2 oz/60 ml) of heated Scotch whisky, set whisky aflame, pour ingredients from one cup to the other several times, thus creating the impression of a con- tinuous stream of fire, then pour into a small heated wineglass, add a slice of lemon or lemon peel, and serve.

BRANDY, GIN, PEACH LIQUEUR, RUM, or WHISKEY GROG

Same preparation as Applejack Grog with the liquor of your choice.

BRANDY, GIN, or WHISKEY SKIN

Same preparation as Columbia Skin with the liquor of your choice.

BRANDY or RUM BLAZER

Same preparation as Blue Blazer with the liquor of your choice.

BRANDY SANGAREE

In a heated tumbler: a teaspoon (4 g) of sugar dissolved in little boiling water, one glass (2 oz/60 ml) of brandy; fill with boiling water and serve with grated nutmeg.

BRANDY SLING

In a heated tumbler: two lumps of sugar dissolved in little boiling

water, a dash (¹⁄₈ tsp/.5 ml) of Angostura bitters, the juice of half a lemon, one glass (2 oz/60 ml) of brandy; add boiling water to suit taste and serve.

COLUMBIA SKIN

In a saucepan: a tablespoon (15 ml) of water, two lumps of sugar (2 tsp/ 8 g), the juice of half a lemon, a teaspoon (5 ml) of curaçao, one glass (2 oz/60 ml) of rum; heat to a simmer, but do not boil; serve in a small heated wineglass.

GIN, PORT, RUM, SHERRY, or WHISKEY SANGAREE

Same preparation as Brandy Sangaree with the liquor of your choice.

GIN, RUM, or WHISKEY SLING

Same preparation as Brandy Sling with the liquor of your choice.

HOT BENEFACTOR

In a heated tumbler: two lumps of sugar dissolved in a little boiling water, one glass (2 oz/60 ml) each of Jamaica rum and red wine; fill with boiling water and serve with a slice of lemon and grated nutmeg if desired.

HOT BRANDY

In a small saucepan: a tablespoon (15 ml) of water, two lumps of sugar (2 tsp/8 g), a pinch of allspice, a small piece of orange peel and one glass (2 oz/60 ml) of brandy; heat to a simmer, but do not boil; set aflame, allow to burn a few seconds, and strain into a small heated wineglass.

HOT GIN, RUM, or WHISKEY

Same preparation as Hot Brandy with the liquor of your choice.

HOT PORT or SHERRY

In small saucepan: a tablespoon (15 ml) of water, one lump of sugar (1 tsp/4 g), a pinch of allspice, a small piece of orange or lemon peel, one glass (2 oz/60 ml) of port or sherry; heat to a simmer, but do not boil; strain into a heated wineglass and serve.

MILK PUNCH

In a heated tumbler: a teaspoon (4 g) of sugar, just enough boiling milk to dissolve the sugar, half a glass (1 oz/30 ml) each of rum and brandy; fill with boiling milk, stir, and serve.

MULLED WINE or HOT CLARET

In small saucepan: two lumps of sugar, one clove, a small piece of cinnamon, a small orange peel or lemon peel, half a pint (8 oz/236 ml) of claret; heat to a simmer, but do not boil; strain into a heated tumbler and serve.

PORT NEGUS

In a small heated tumbler: one lump of sugar dissolved in a little boiling water, one glass (2 oz/60 ml) of red port; add boiling water until desired temperature is reached, grate nutmeg on top, and serve.

SHERRY NEGUS

Same preparation as Port Negus, except with sweet sherry.

SPICED RUM

In a small heated tumbler: two lumps of sugar dissolved in a little boiling water, a pinch of allspice, one glass (2 oz/60 ml) of rum, a small piece of butter; fill with boiling waiter, stir, and serve.

TOM & JERRY
FOR ABOUT FIFTY DRINKS

Take twelve eggs, beating the whites and yolks separately; mix together in a large bowl, add a teaspoon (2 g) of allspice, one bottle of rum, and one pound (450 g) of powdered sugar; stir thoroughly to thicken. How to serve Tom & Jerry: in a large heated cup or tumbler, pour in a tablespoon (15 ml) of the above mixture, half a glass (1 oz/30 ml) of brandy: fill with boiling milk while stirring to a foam, grate nutmeg on top, and serve. (Boiling water may be used instead of boiling milk, if preferred.)

If the boiling water added is not enough to heat the drink sufficiently, the ingredients may be heated together in a small saucepan.

MISCELLANEOUS DRINKS

AMERICAN BEAUTY

In a large tumbler: a teaspoon (5 ml) each of white crème de menthe and grenadine, the juice of half an orange, half a glass (1 oz/30 ml) each of French vermouth and brandy; fill with shaved ice, stir, decorate with seasonal fruit and a sprig of mint, top with red port, and serve with straws and spoon.

AMERICAN ROSE

In a shaker: a dash (⅛ tsp/.5 ml) of absinthe, a teaspoon (5 ml) of grenadine, half a glass (1 oz/30 ml) of brandy, two slices of ripe peach or pear crushed in a shaker with a fork; shake well, strain into a tumbler, fill with champagne, and serve.

AMERICANO

In a tumbler or large wineglass: a piece of ice, one glass (2 oz/60 ml) each of Campari and Italian vermouth; add a lemon peel, top with soda water, stir, and serve.

ANGOSTURA & GINGER ALE

In a tumbler: a large piece of ice, a teaspoon (5 ml) of Angostura bitters, fill with ginger ale, stir, and serve.

ANGOSTURA & SODA

In a tumbler: a large piece of ice, a teaspoon (5 ml) of Angostura bitters, half a teaspoon (2 g) of sugar, fill with soda water, stir, and serve.

BARBOTAGE OF CHAMPAGNE

In a tumbler half filled with cracked ice: a dash (⅛ tsp/.5 ml) of Angostura bitters, a teaspoon (5 ml) each of lemon juice and simple syrup; fill with champagne, stir, add an orange slice, and serve.

BARMAN'S DELIGHT

"Just a little whiskey, straight if you please."

(From *The World's Drinks and How to Mix Them*)*

BISHOP

In a tumbler half filled with cracked ice: a teaspoon (4 g) of sugar, the juices of half a lemon and half an orange; fill with red Burgundy or claret, stir, add an orange slice, a dash (⅛ tsp/.5 ml) of rum, and serve.

BISMARCK or BLACK VELVET

Into a large tumbler with a piece of ice, slowly pour a bottle of Guinness stout and add an equal amount of champagne; stir gently and serve.

*Manual by the famous bartender William "Cocktail" Boothby, published in 1900.

BLACK ROSE

In a tumbler: a large piece of ice, a teaspoon (4 g) of sugar, half a glass (1 oz/30 ml) of St. James rum; fill with cold black coffee, stir, and serve.

BLACK STRIPE

In a cocktail glass: a teaspoon (5 ml) of molasses; fill with rum, stir, and serve.

BORDEAUX CHAMPAGNE

In a tumbler: a piece of ice, half (1 oz/30 ml) claret, half (1 oz/30 ml) champagne; stir and serve.

BOSOM CARESSER

In a shaker: one egg yolk, a dash (1/8 tsp/.5 ml) of grenadine, a dash (1/8 tsp/.5 ml) of curaçao, half a glass (1 oz/30 ml) each of brandy and Madeira; shake well, strain into a double cocktail glass, and serve.

BRANDY & HONEY

In a small tumbler: a piece of ice, a teaspoon (5 ml) of honey, leaving spoon in the tumbler, one glass (2 oz/60 ml) of brandy; stir and serve with a glass of water.

BRANDY, GIN, or WHISKEY SKIN

Same preparation as Columbia Skin with the liquor of your choice.

BYRRH CASSIS

In a tumbler or large wineglass: a piece of ice, a teaspoon (5 ml) of crème de cassis, one glass (2 oz/60 ml) of Byrrh; top with soda water and serve.

CAFÉ & KIRSCH—COLD

In a tumbler: two or three pieces of ice, half a glass (1 oz/30 ml) of kirsch; fill with cold black coffee, stir, and serve with powdered sugar if desired.

CASSISCO

A popular French drink. In a tumbler or large wineglass: a piece of ice, a tablespoon (15 ml) of crème de cassis, half a glass (1 oz/30 ml) of brandy; top with soda water, stir, and serve.

CHAMBÉRY FRAISE

In a tumbler or large wineglass: a piece of ice, a teaspoon (5 ml) of strawberry syrup, one glass (2 oz/60 ml) of Chambéry vermouth; top with soda water, stir, and serve.

COLUMBIA SKIN

In a shaker: a teaspoon (4 g) of sugar, the juice of half a lemon, a teaspoon (5 ml) of curaçao, one glass (2 oz/60 ml) of rum: shake well, strain into a small wineglass, and serve.

CORPSE REVIVER nº 2   ◈

In a tumbler: a piece of ice, the juice of a quarter lemon, one glass (2 oz/60 ml) of pastis; fill with champagne, stir, and serve.

DOG'S NOSE

In a tumbler: half a bottle of stout, a dash (1/8 tsp/.5 ml) of gin, and serve.

DUBONNET CITRON

In a tumbler or large wineglass: a piece of ice, a tablespoon (15 ml) of lemon syrup, one glass (2oz/60 ml) of Dubonnet; top with soda water and serve.

ESKIMO

In a shaker: a tablespoon (10 g) of vanilla ice cream, a dash (⅛ tsp/ .5 ml) each of curaçao and maraschino, one glass (2 oz/60 ml) of brandy; shake well, strain into a wineglass, and serve with a spoon and straws.

EYE OPENER

In a shaker: one egg yolk, half a glass (1 oz/30 ml) each of curaçao, rum, and pastis; shake well, strain into a fizz glass, and serve.

FOGHORN

In a tumbler: a large piece of ice, one glass (2 oz/60 ml) of gin, fill with ginger beer, add a slice of lemon, and serve.

FRANK'S REFRESHER

In a large tumbler: two or three pieces of ice, the juice of half a lemon, half a glass (1 oz/30 ml) each of raspberry or strawberry syrup and brandy; fill with champagne, stir, and serve.

GIN BUCK

In a tumbler: a large piece of ice, the juice of half a lime or a quarter lemon, one glass (2 oz/60 ml) of gin; top with ginger ale, stir, and serve.

GIN SPIDER

In a tumbler: a large piece of ice, a dash (⅛ tsp/.5 ml) of Angostura bitters, one glass (2 oz/60ml) of gin; top with ginger ale, stir, and serve.

GIN & TONIC

In a tumbler: a large piece of ice, one glass of gin (2 oz/60 ml), a slice of lemon; fill with Indian Tonic, stir, and serve.

GOLDEN FLEECE

In a cocktail glass half filled with shaved ice: half (1 oz/30 ml) yellow Chartreuse, half (1 oz/30 ml) Danziger Goldwasser. An after-dinner drink.

GREEN HAT ◈

In a tumbler: a large piece of ice, half a glass (1 oz/30 ml) each of gin and green crème de menthe; top with soda water, stir, and serve.

GRENADINE & KIRSCH

In a tumbler or large wineglass: a piece of ice, half a glass (1 oz/30 ml) each of kirsch and grenadine; top with soda water, stir, and serve.

HORSE'S NECK

In a large tumbler: two pieces of ice a whole lemon rind; fill with ginger ale, stir, and serve. Half a glass (1 oz/30ml) of brandy, gin, rum, or whiskey may be added if desired.

IRISH ROSE

In a shaker: the juice of half a lemon, a teaspoon (5 ml) of grenadine, one glass (2 oz/60 ml) of Irish whiskey; shake well, strain into a fizz glass, and serve.

KING'S PEG or BRANDY & CHAMPAGNE

In a large wineglass: a piece of ice, half a glass (1 oz/30 ml) of brandy; fill with champagne, and serve.

KOLDKURE ◈

In a cocktail glass: a teaspoon (5 ml) of grenadine, the juice of a quarter lemon, fill with rum; stir and serve. A good remedy for a cold.

MACKA

A popular French drink. In a tumbler half filled with cracked ice: a dash (1/8 tsp/.5 ml) of crème de cassis, one-third (1 oz/30 ml) each of gin, French vermouth, and Italian vermouth; stir well, add a slice of orange, and serve.

MAGNOLIA

In a shaker: one egg yolk, a teaspoon (5 ml) of curaçao, half a glass (1 oz/30 ml) of brandy; shake well, strain into a fizz glass, fill with champagne, and serve.

MAMY TAYLOR

In a large tumbler: a piece of ice, a slice of lemon, one glass (2 oz/60 ml) of gin; fill with ginger ale, stir, and serve.

MIMOSA or CHAMPAGNE ORANGE

In a large wineglass: a piece of ice, the juice of half an orange; fill with champagne, stir, and serve.

MORNING BRACER

In a shaker: a dash (1/8 tsp/.5 ml) of Angostura bitters, half a glass (1 oz/30 ml) each of pastis and French vermouth; shake well, strain into a double cocktail glass, top with soda water, and serve.

MORNING SMILE

In a shaker: one fresh egg, half a teaspoon (2 g) of sugar, one glass (2 oz/60 ml) of bourbon whiskey, one glass (2 oz/60 ml) of fresh milk; shake well, strain into a tumbler, and serve.

PEACH BRANDY & HONEY, RUM & HONEY, or WHISKEY & HONEY

Same preparation as Brandy & Honey with the liquor of your choice.

PICK-ME-UP

In a shaker: a dash (1/8 tsp/.5 ml) of Angostura bitters, a teaspoon (4 g) of sugar, one glass (2 oz/60 ml) of brandy, one glass (2 oz/60 ml) of fresh milk; shake well, strain into a tumbler, top with soda water, and serve.

PICON-GRENADINE

In a tumbler or large wineglass: a piece of ice, one glass (2 oz/60 ml) of Amer Picon, a teaspoon (5 ml) of grenadine; top with soda water, stir, and serve.

PRINCE OF WALES

In a shaker: a dash (1/8 tsp/.5 ml) of Angostura bitters, a teaspoon (5 ml) of curaçao, half a glass (1 oz/30 ml) each of Madeira and brandy; shake well, strain into a large wineglass, fill with champagne, add a slice of orange, and serve.

QUEEN'S PEG or GIN & CHAMPAGNE

In a large wineglass: a piece of ice, half a glass (1 oz/30 ml) of gin; fill with champagne and serve.

RAINBOW

Into a tall liqueur glass or pousse-café glass, pour slowly and carefully the following ingredients on top of one another using a barspoon or round teaspoon, holding the spoon against the inside of the glass:

Pastis rosé	pink
Mint	green
Chartreuse	yellow
Cherry brandy	red
Kümmel	white
Chartreuse	green
Cognac brandy	brown

Use quantities of liqueurs according to the size and shape of the glass, so that all the stripes of color are of equal height.

RHINE WINE or MOSELLE & SELTZER

In a tumbler: two-thirds (2 oz/ 60 ml) of chilled Rhine or Moselle wine, one-third (1 oz/30 ml) of cold soda water and serve.

ROCK & RYE

In a small tumbler: a piece of crushed rock candy or a teaspoon (5 ml) of cane sugar syrup, leaving the spoon in the tumbler, one glass

(2 oz/60 ml) of rye whiskey; a few drops of lemon juice, if desired, and serve with a glass of ice water.

SHANDY GAFF

In a large tumbler: half (6 oz/180 ml) cold pale ale, half (6 oz/180 ml) cold ginger ale; stir gently and serve.

SHERRY & EGG

In a cocktail glass: a dash (⅛ tsp/ .5 ml) of sherry, one egg yolk; fill with sherry and serve. Or, in a cocktail glass half filled with sherry, drop one egg yolk and serve.

SOYER AU CHAMPAGNE

In a tumbler half filled with cracked ice: a tablespoon (15 ml) of orange juice, a teaspoon (5 ml) each of maraschino and brandy; fill with champagne, stir, add an orange slice and seasonal fruit, and serve with a spoon.

STONE FENCE

In a tumbler: a large piece of ice, one glass (2 oz/60 ml) of bourbon or rye whiskey; fill with sweet cider, stir, and serve.

STONE WALL

In a tumbler: a large piece of ice, half a teaspoon (2 g) of sugar, one glass (2 oz/60 ml) of Scotch whisky, top with soda water, stir, and serve.

TOMATE

A popular French drink. In a tumbler or large wineglass: a piece of ice, one glass (2 oz/60 ml) of pastis, a teaspoon (5 ml) of grenadine; add water to suit taste, stir, and serve.

VERMOUTH CASSIS

A popular French drink. In a tumbler or large wineglass: a piece of ice, one glass (2 oz/60 ml) of French vermouth, a tablespoon (15 ml) of cassis syrup; top with soda water, stir, and serve.

WHITE PLUSH

In a tumbler: a piece of ice, one glass (2 oz/60 ml) of bourbon or rye whiskey; fill with fresh milk and serve.

NONALCOHOLIC DRINKS

CLAM JUICE COCKTAIL
In a shaker: a teaspoon (5 ml) of ketchup, a small pinch of celery salt, two or three drops of Tabasco sauce, one glass (2 oz/60 ml) of clam juice; shake slightly and serve.

GRAPE JUICE CUP
FOR TEN DRINKS
In a half-gallon pitcher (about 2 L): a lump of ice, the juice of six lemons, one glass (2 oz/60 ml) of grenadine, one quart (1 L) of grape juice; top with soda water, add seasonal berries, stir, and serve.

ICED CHOCOLATE
In a large tumbler half filled with cracked ice: very thick hot chocolate to fill glass; stir slightly and serve with a little milk or cream, if desired.

ICED COFFEE

In a large tumbler half filled with cracked ice: a teaspoon (4 g) of sugar, very strong black coffee to fill glass; stir slightly and serve with a little milk or cream, if desired.

ICED TEA

In a large tumbler two-thirds full of cracked ice: a teaspoon (4 g) of sugar, very strong tea to fill glass; stir until cold, add slice of lemon, and serve.

MILK & SELTZER or
MILK & VICHY

In a tumbler: one-third (1 oz/ 30 ml) cold seltzer or Vichy sparkling water, fresh milk to fill glass, and serve.

ORGEAT FIZZ

In a shaker: the juice of half a lemon, one glass (2 oz/60 ml) of orgeat (almond syrup); shake well, strain into a fizz glass, top with soda water, and serve.

PARISETTE

In a tumbler: a piece of ice, a tablespoon (15 ml) of grenadine; fill with fresh milk, stir, and serve.

ROSEY SQUASH

In a tumbler: a large piece of ice, the juice of half a lemon, a tablespoon (15 ml) of grenadine; top with soda water, stir, and serve.

SUMMER DELIGHT

In a large tumbler: two or three pieces of ice, the juice of one lime or half a lemon, half a glass (2 oz/60 ml) of raspberry syrup; top with soda water, stir, add seasonal fruit, and serve with a spoon.

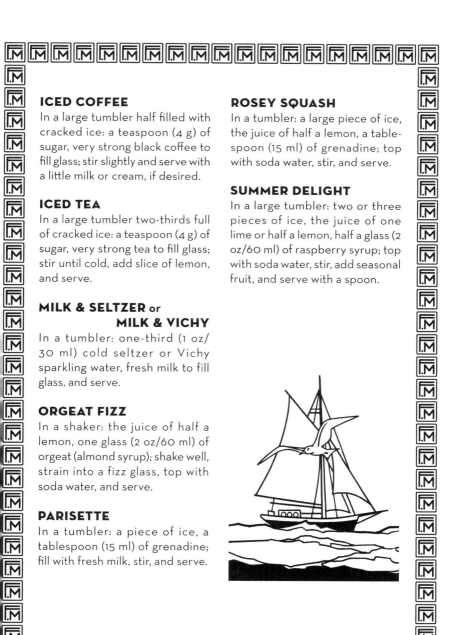

III.
SANDWICHES

Said to have been named after John Montagu, the 4th Earl of Sandwich (died 1792), consisting of two thin slices of buttered bread with some savory food in between.

ANCHOVY

Chop three boned anchovies and a hard-boiled egg, add a piece of butter, pound together until smooth, use as filling between slices of white or brown bread and butter (for two sandwiches). Sardines may be used instead of anchovies.

APPLE & CHEESE

Chop a large apple into very fine pieces, grate the same amount of Cheshire cheese, moisten with a little melted butter, spread on slices of buttered brown bread (for three sandwiches).

BANANA & CHEESE

Mash a banana, add lemon juice to suit taste, spread slices of brown bread and butter with soft cheese, and sandwich together with banana mixture (for two sandwiches).

BEEF

On white bread or rolls, spread butter mixed with a very small amount of grated horseradish, lay thin slices of beef or beef tongue (roasted, pressed, salted, corned, spiced, or chipped) on half of the prepared bread or rolls, add mustard, salt, and pepper to suit taste, and cover with the remaining pieces of bread or rolls.

CAVIAR

Cut and butter thin slices of white or brown bread, spread a thin layer of caviar on half of them, then sprinkle with a small amount of cayenne pepper, a little lemon juice, or some very finely chopped onion, and cover with the remaining slices of bread.

CHEESE

Butter toast, saltine crackers, water crackers, or any bread; cover with grated or soft cheese, salt and pepper, cayenne pepper, or mustard.

CHEESE & EGG

Chop a hard-boiled egg, add an equal amount of grated cheese, enough melted butter, season with a little cayenne, salt, and a dash (1/8 tsp/.5 ml) of Worcestershire sauce, spread a layer between buttered slices of white or brown bread (for two sandwiches).

CHEESE ON CRACKERS

Place a square slice of Cheshire cheese on a saltine cracker, sprinkle with a little cayenne pepper, and grill.

CHESTNUT & CHEESE

Chop a few grilled chestnuts into very small pieces, add an equal amount of soft cheese, moisten with a little heavy cream and season to taste; spread between buttered slices of white or brown bread.

CHICKEN & CELERY

Chop up cooked chicken (white meat) and half the amount of raw celery, moisten with mayonnaise, season to taste, and use as filling for buttered white bread or rolls.

CHICKEN & HAM

Chop up cooked chicken and half the amount of cooked ham, add a very small amount of finely chopped parsley, moisten with a little heavy cream, season to taste and spread between buttered slices of white or brown bread.

CLUB

Split a thick piece of hot toast in two, then butter both sides and fill with four small slices of grilled bacon, white chicken meat, chopped lettuce mixed with mayonnaise, slices of tomatoes, and salt and pepper. Heat slightly in the oven or under the grill.

CRAB

Mash up some crabmeat, moisten with salad dressing, season to taste, and put between buttered slices of white or brown bread, adding a few very thin slices of cucumber. Lobster or shrimp may be used instead of crabmeat.

CRAB & EGG

Chop a hard-boiled egg and some crabmeat, moisten with mayonnaise and a few drops of lemon juice or vinegar; place between slices of buttered brown bread.

DEVILED TOAST

Mix a tablespoon (14 g) of butter with a teaspoon (5 g) each of English and French mustard, chutney, curry powder, cayenne pepper, lemon juice, and a little salt; spread on toast and heat in the oven or under the grill.

EGG & LETTUCE

Chop up a hard-boiled egg, enough lettuce for two sandwiches, moisten with mayonnaise, and season to taste; place between buttered slices of white bread.

EGG & WATERCRESS

Chop up a hard-boiled egg and enough watercress for two sandwiches, moisten with salad dressing, add salt to suit taste; place between buttered slices of white or brown bread. Cucumber sliced or chopped tomato may be used instead of watercress.

FISH (SAVORY)*

Heat slightly some leftover cooked fish, mince with some very finely chopped parsley, season with an appropriate piquant sauce, spread on thin fried or buttered toast, put under the grill; sprinkle with a little lemon juice and serve very hot.

FOIE GRAS

Pound together foie gras and half the quantity of butter, a few drops of Worcestershire sauce, salt and pepper; spread between saltines, water crackers, sliced bread, rolls, or English muffins.

GAME

Chop up cooked game, moisten with a brown piquant sauce, add a very small amount of currant jelly or other sweet jelly; spread between buttered slices of white bread.

GORGONZOLA or ROQUEFORT

Using a table fork, pound together Gorgonzola or Roquefort cheese with butter and some very finely chopped celery, add a few drops of Worcestershire sauce and a little cayenne pepper; spread a thickish layer on slices of white or brown bread.

HAM & CELERY

Chop up cooked ham and half the amount of celery, moisten with a little cream, add ketchup and a very small amount of cayenne pepper; spread between small, buttered rolls. Can be served hot by heating filled rolls in the oven.

HAM & CHEESE

Use toast or any sliced bread; butter, lay a few thin slices of cooked ham, cover with thin slices of Gruyère or Swiss cheese, add mustard, chutney, or ketchup, and assemble the sandwich.

*Dish to be served at the end of the meal, just before . . . or after dessert! These bites were
  very appreciated in the Edwardian era.

LOBSTER & EGG: see CRAB & EGG

MUSHROOM—HOT
Slice a thick piece of toasted bread in two, fill with four fresh grilled mushrooms and two slices of bacon, heat again in the oven or under the grill.

PORK or VEAL
Cover buttered slices of bread with slices of roast pork or veal, salt, and pepper, add chutney or piquant sauce and assemble the sandwich.

RADISH
Butter slices of white or brown bread, cut and mince radishes, moisten with mayonnaise or a thick salad dressing; sandwich together with grated or soft cheese.

SARDINE
Butter thin slices of white bread, split two sardines in half and remove the skin and bones, put the four halves on prepared bread, sprinkle with cayenne pepper and very finely chopped parsley, and assemble the sandwich.

SARDINE—HOT
Slice a thick piece of toasted bread in two, split two sardines in half and remove the skin and bones, put the four halves on each piece of toast, sprinkle with a very small amount of cayenne pepper, and heat in the oven or under the grill.

SAUSAGE
Grill or fry two small pork sausages, split a hot roll in half, add mustard, place sausages in roll; serve hot.

SHRIMP & EGG: see CRAB & EGG

SMOKED SALMON

Butter thin slices of white or brown bread, lay thin slices of smoked salmon on half the pieces, sprinkle with a little lemon juice and cayenne pepper, then cover with remaining bread and press together.

TOMATO

Spread butter mixed with finely grated horseradish on white bread, lay thin slices of peeled but not too ripe tomatoes, salt, and pepper to suit taste, and assemble the sandwich.

TUNA FISH

Chop some canned tuna fish and a little parsley, mix well with highly seasoned salad dressing; use as a filling between buttered slices of white or brown bread, adding a very small amount of finely chopped onion or celery.

TURKEY

Pound together turkey (white meat), smoked beef tongue, and celery until smooth, then add a little mayonnaise, salt and pepper; spread on slices of white or brown buttered bread and assemble the sandwich. Chicken may be used instead of turkey.

TURKEY & CRANBERRY

Spread cranberry sauce or jelly on buttered slices of white or brown bread, lay thin slices of turkey (white meat) on half the bread, and cover with the other buttered slices of bread.

WELSH RAREBIT

Use toasted and buttered English muffin or tender toasted bread, cover with a thick layer of grated Gloucester or Cheshire cheese, sprinkle with a little salt and cayenne pepper, put under the grill, and serve hot. The original recipe consists of putting small pieces of cheese and some ale in a saucepan, adding a few drops of Worcestershire sauce, cayenne, and mustard, cooking slightly, and pouring the mixture over hot buttered toast.

IV.
WINES &
SPIRITS

**If God forbade us from drinking, would
he have made wine so good?**

Wine is justly considered the most wholesome of beverages. And 1934 has been, according to official figures, the greatest wine-producing year yet known. It is therefore of interest to write about it. The thirty-eight wine-growing countries* are mentioned below: Algeria, Argentine, Australia, Austria, the Azores and Canary Islands, Bolivia, Brazil, Bulgaria, Canada, Chili, Corsica, Czecho-Slovakia, Egypt, Germany, Greece and its islands, Hungary, Italy, Jugo-Slavia, Luxemburg, Madeira, Mexico, Morocco, Palestine, Peru, Portugal, Rumania and Bessarabia, Russia, South Africa, Spain, Switzerland, Tunisia, Turkey and Cyprus, U.S. of America, Uruguay, and France, have actually produced the impressive amount of 100,000,000,000 (one hundred billion) bottles, about five times the quantity of 1933.

Grapes will grow wherever there is a little sun. Since Caesar and the early Christian fathers discovered that the climate and soil of France produced superlatively fine wine, the French have made the best of ideal conditions until pure winemaking has become an art in which they excel. They have proved that "years" are real tests of quality. No people more than the wine growers of Bordeaux, Burgundy, and Champagne would like to have all years be "great years." The next best thing to annual "great years" is purity and naturalness. This is what French wine producers insist on. A good wine merchant, a good wine butler, or a good bartender will always recommend an authentic French wine.

*The names of the countries listed have been transcribed as written by the author, without being updated.

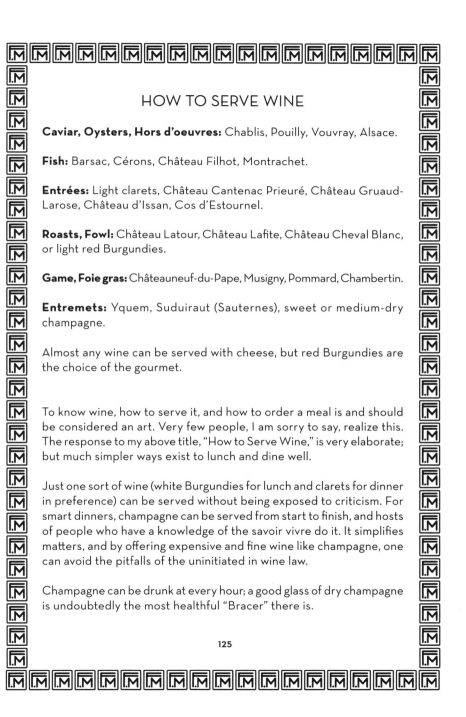

HOW TO SERVE WINE

Caviar, Oysters, Hors d'oeuvres: Chablis, Pouilly, Vouvray, Alsace.

Fish: Barsac, Cérons, Château Filhot, Montrachet.

Entrées: Light clarets, Château Cantenac Prieuré, Château Gruaud-Larose, Château d'Issan, Cos d'Estournel.

Roasts, Fowl: Château Latour, Château Lafite, Château Cheval Blanc, or light red Burgundies.

Game, Foie gras: Châteauneuf-du-Pape, Musigny, Pommard, Chambertin.

Entremets: Yquem, Suduiraut (Sauternes), sweet or medium-dry champagne.

Almost any wine can be served with cheese, but red Burgundies are the choice of the gourmet.

To know wine, how to serve it, and how to order a meal is and should be considered an art. Very few people, I am sorry to say, realize this. The response to my above title, "How to Serve Wine," is very elaborate; but much simpler ways exist to lunch and dine well.

Just one sort of wine (white Burgundies for lunch and clarets for dinner in preference) can be served without being exposed to criticism. For smart dinners, champagne can be served from start to finish, and hosts of people who have a knowledge of the savoir vivre do it. It simplifies matters, and by offering expensive and fine wine like champagne, one can avoid the pitfalls of the uninitiated in wine law.

Champagne can be drunk at every hour; a good glass of dry champagne is undoubtedly the most healthful "Bracer" there is.

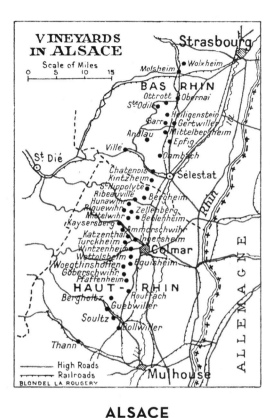

ALSACE

Since the Great War, no effort has been spared to bring up Alsatian wines to the reputation of the German Hocks and Moselles. The towns and such typical villages as Marlenheim, Wolxheim, Obernai, Molsheim, Heiligenstein, Otrott, Barr, Gertwiller, Mittelbergheim, Andlau, Dambach, Châtenois, Kintzheim, Saint-Hippolyte, Bergheim, Ribeauvillé, Hunawihr, Zellenberg, Beblenheim, Riquewihr, Mittelwihr, Kientzheim, Kaysersberg, Ammerschwihr, Katzenthal, Ingersheim, Türckheim,

Wintzenheim, Colmar, Eguisheim, Wettolsheim, Woegtlinshoffen, Goberschwihr, Pfaffenheim, Rouffach, Guebwiller, Soultz, Thann, and many others, surrounded as they are by beautiful vineyards along the wide Rhine valley, from Strasburg up as far as Thann and Mulhouse, produce those excellent and characteristic wines called Riesling, Traminer, Gewürztraminer, Kitterlé, Sporen, Clos Sainte Odile, Klevner, Gentil, Sylvaner, Rangen, Knipperlé, Chasselas, Zwicker, etc.

Most of them are fairly dry, with an exquisite and peculiar bouquet, and are very popular luncheon wines.

Kindly contributed to the author by Pierre Freyburger.

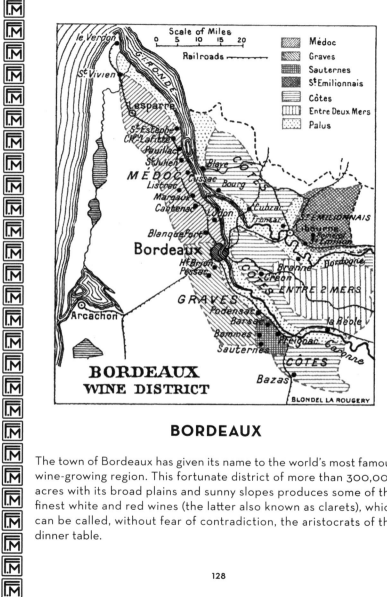

BORDEAUX WINE DISTRICT

BORDEAUX

The town of Bordeaux has given its name to the world's most famous wine-growing region. This fortunate district of more than 300,000 acres with its broad plains and sunny slopes produces some of the finest white and red wines (the latter also known as clarets), which can be called, without fear of contradiction, the aristocrats of the dinner table.

Of the seven regions—Médoc, Graves, Sauternes, Saint-Émilionnais, Côtes, Palus, Entre-Deux-Mers—Médoc is the home of Château Lafite, Château Latour, Château Margaux, to speak only of first growths; Graves, of the Château Haut-Brion; Sauternes, of the Château Yquem (white); Saint-Émilionnais, of the Château Cheval Blanc. Besides these very exceptional products, sixteen *deuxièmes crus*, fourteen *troisièmes crus*, ten *quatrièmes crus*, seventeen *cinquièmes crus* also belong to the classified growths. Then come another 1,359 *châteaux*, *domaines*, and *clos* (1,421 in all) that produce the huge quantities of Bordeaux wines, red and white, here mentioned:

Year	Quality	Bottles	Year	Quality	Bottles
1900	Very good	716,625,000	1918	Good	470,250,000
1901	Fair	537,750,000	1919	Very good	636,975,000
1902	Poor	357,750,000	1920	Very good	608,748,750
1903	Fairly good	262,125,000	1921	Uneven (good)	480,500,000
1904	Perfect	562,500,000	1922	Light, excellent	899,087,500
1905	Good	536,850,000	1923	Good	614,250,000
1906	Good	437,625,000	1924	Very good	700,675,000
1907	Uneven	686,250,000	1925	Fair	644,734,250
1908	Fair	405,000,000	1926	Good	487,497,750
1909	Good	468,000,000	1927	Fair	501,506,000
1910	Disastrous	191,250,000	1928	Very good	589,727,125
1911	Good	399,936,500	1929	Remarkable	571,715,750
1912	Good	519,432,750	1930	Mediocre	318,688,625
1913	Good	412,875,000	1931	Fair	478,257,750
1914	Very good	668,137,500	1932	Poor	478,455,250
1915	Very poor	153,900,000	1933	Poor	421,052,750
1916	Good	381,037,500	1934	Good	855,473,125
1917	Light, but good	442,237,500	1935	Good	527,974,800

In 1934, France, without its colonies,* produced 75,143,622 hectoliters, or 9,392,952,750 bottles of wine, against 49,690,687 hectoliters in 1933.

*Readers should recall that Frank Meier's original book was published in 1936.

BOURGOGNE

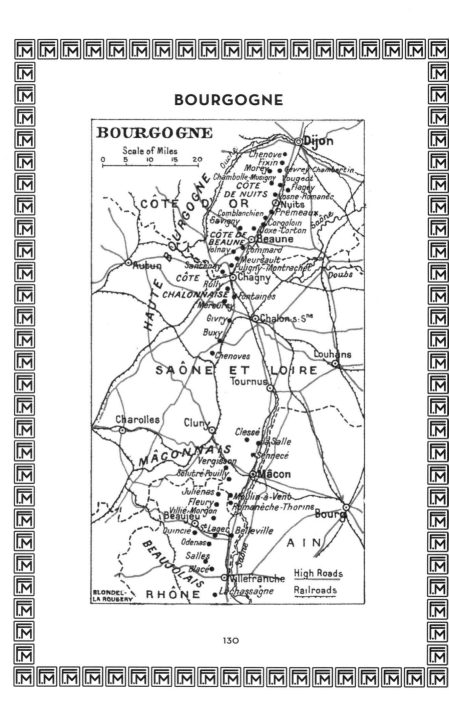

BOURGOGNE

Scale of Miles
0   5   10   15   20

Dijon
Chenove
Fixin
Morey   Gevrey-Chambertin
Chambolle-Musigny   Vougeot
CÔTE   Flagey
DE NUITS   Vosne-Romanée
CÔTE D'OR   Nuits
Prémeaux
Comblanchien
Savigny   Corgoloin
Aloxe-Corton
CÔTE DE   Beaune
BEAUNE
Volnay   Pommard
Meursault
Santenay   Puligny-Montrachet
CÔTE   Rully   Chagny
CHALONNAISE   Fontaines
Mercurey
Givry   Chalon.s.Sne
Buxy
Chenoves   Louhans
SAÔNE   ET   LOIRE
Tournus
Charolles   Cluny
Clessé
MÂCONNAIS   la Salle
Vergisson   Sennecé
Solutré-Pouilly   Mâcon
Juliénas   Moulin-à-Vent
Fleury   Romanèche-Thorins
Villié-Morgon   Bourg
Beaujeu
Quincié   St.Lager   Belleville
Odenas   AIN
BEAUJOLAIS   Salles
Blacé
Villefranche   High Roads
BLONDEL-   la Chassagne   Railroads
LA ROUSERY   RHÔNE

HAUTE BOURGOGNE
Autun
Doubs
Ouche
Saône

Burgundy comprises a region about one hundred eighty miles long and in some places almost sixty miles wide. It produces the greatest, rarest, and probably the most imitated of wines.

Although not officially classified (like Bordeaux wines), Burgundies have always been considered as the kings of all wines. The Côte de Dijon, the Côte de Nuits and Côte de Beaune (Côte d'Or or Golden Hills), and the Côte Chalonnaise produce in an average good year about 300,000,000 bottles, and, without any exaggeration, ten times that amount of wine is sold throughout the world under the name of Burgundy from France.

The Rhone Valley (Côtes du Rhone) also produces excellent red and white wines. The outstanding brands are Côte Rôtie, Hermitage, Châteauneuf-du-Pape, Château-Grillet, and Tavel (rosé).

131

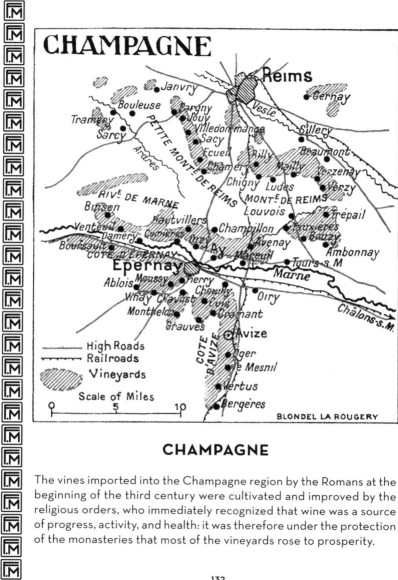

CHAMPAGNE

The vines imported into the Champagne region by the Romans at the beginning of the third century were cultivated and improved by the religious orders, who immediately recognized that wine was a source of progress, activity, and health: it was therefore under the protection of the monasteries that most of the vineyards rose to prosperity.

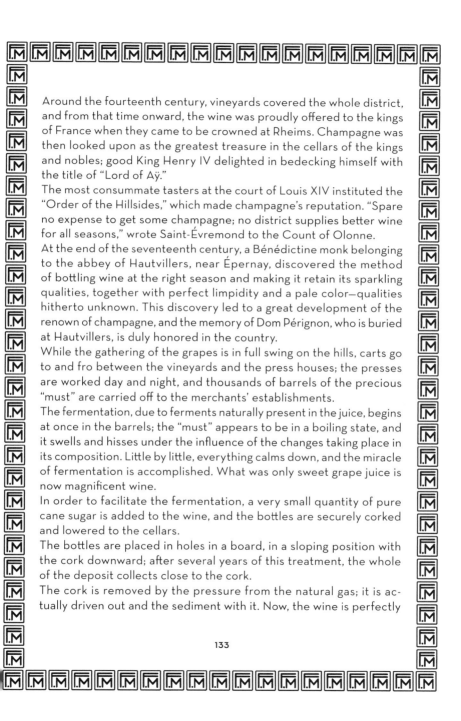

Around the fourteenth century, vineyards covered the whole district, and from that time onward, the wine was proudly offered to the kings of France when they came to be crowned at Rheims. Champagne was then looked upon as the greatest treasure in the cellars of the kings and nobles; good King Henry IV delighted in bedecking himself with the title of "Lord of Aÿ."

The most consummate tasters at the court of Louis XIV instituted the "Order of the Hillsides," which made champagne's reputation. "Spare no expense to get some champagne; no district supplies better wine for all seasons," wrote Saint-Évremond to the Count of Olonne.

At the end of the seventeenth century, a Bénédictine monk belonging to the abbey of Hautvillers, near Épernay, discovered the method of bottling wine at the right season and making it retain its sparkling qualities, together with perfect limpidity and a pale color—qualities hitherto unknown. This discovery led to a great development of the renown of champagne, and the memory of Dom Pérignon, who is buried at Hautvillers, is duly honored in the country.

While the gathering of the grapes is in full swing on the hills, carts go to and fro between the vineyards and the press houses; the presses are worked day and night, and thousands of barrels of the precious "must" are carried off to the merchants' establishments.

The fermentation, due to ferments naturally present in the juice, begins at once in the barrels; the "must" appears to be in a boiling state, and it swells and hisses under the influence of the changes taking place in its composition. Little by little, everything calms down, and the miracle of fermentation is accomplished. What was only sweet grape juice is now magnificent wine.

In order to facilitate the fermentation, a very small quantity of pure cane sugar is added to the wine, and the bottles are securely corked and lowered to the cellars.

The bottles are placed in holes in a board, in a sloping position with the cork downward; after several years of this treatment, the whole of the deposit collects close to the cork.

The cork is removed by the pressure from the natural gas; it is actually driven out and the sediment with it. Now, the wine is perfectly limpid. Before recorking the bottle, the necessary sweetening is affected by adding still more pure cane sugar dissolved in champagne of the best quality. The object of this is to meet the taste of the consumer, who, according to different countries, may prefer wines more or less sweetened.

Before shipping, the bottle is "dressed" with a capsule and label bearing the name of the firm and the word "champagne," which is a legal guarantee of its origin.

The district authorized by French law to give the name of champagne to its wine is small compared with other wine-growing regions. The nature of the soil, the sorts of vine grown, and the special methods of cultivation in use result in the production of a high quality at the sacrifice of quantity; here, as elsewhere, quality is scarcely compatible with quantity.

The crop varies considerably from year to year and can only be estimated by taking an average over a long period. For thirty normal years, the average production was 450,000 hectoliters or about 10,000,000 gallons a year, i.e., 60,000,000 bottles.

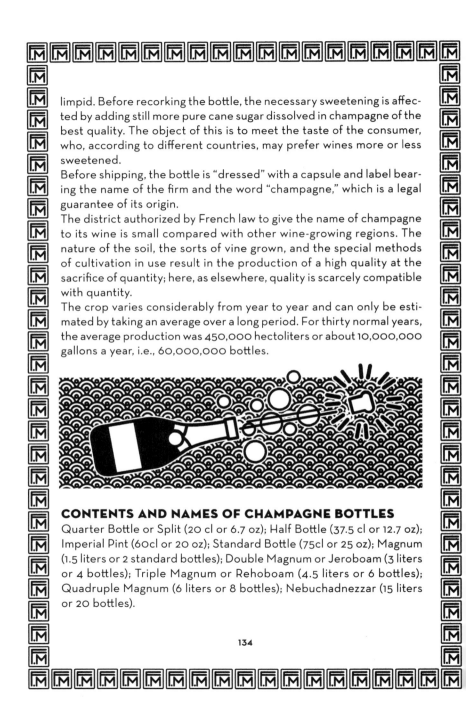

CONTENTS AND NAMES OF CHAMPAGNE BOTTLES

Quarter Bottle or Split (20 cl or 6.7 oz); Half Bottle (37.5 cl or 12.7 oz); Imperial Pint (60cl or 20 oz); Standard Bottle (75cl or 25 oz); Magnum (1.5 liters or 2 standard bottles); Double Magnum or Jeroboam (3 liters or 4 bottles); Triple Magnum or Rehoboam (4.5 liters or 6 bottles); Quadruple Magnum (6 liters or 8 bottles); Nebuchadnezzar (15 liters or 20 bottles).

SAUMUR

A tour of the châteaux of Touraine is incomplete without a visit to Saumur, a pleasant town, built in a picturesque position between the Loire and the Thouet. On the banks of the Thouet is the village of Saint-Hilaire-Saint-Florent, with curious caves hollowed out of the hillside. This is the center of the sparkling wine industry of Saumur, founded by Jean Ackerman in 1811.

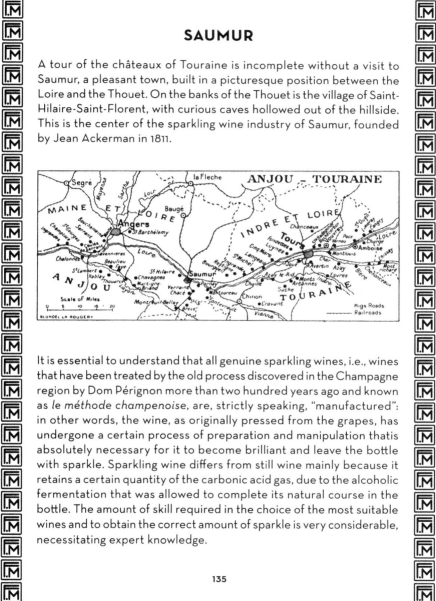

It is essential to understand that all genuine sparkling wines, i.e., wines that have been treated by the old process discovered in the Champagne region by Dom Pérignon more than two hundred years ago and known as *le méthode champenoise*, are, strictly speaking, "manufactured": in other words, the wine, as originally pressed from the grapes, has undergone a certain process of preparation and manipulation that is absolutely necessary for it to become brilliant and leave the bottle with sparkle. Sparkling wine differs from still wine mainly because it retains a certain quantity of the carbonic acid gas, due to the alcoholic fermentation that was allowed to complete its natural course in the bottle. The amount of skill required in the choice of the most suitable wines and to obtain the correct amount of sparkle is very considerable, necessitating expert knowledge.

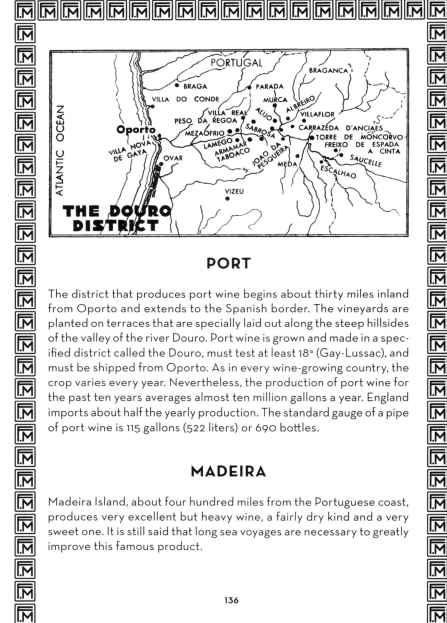

THE DOURO
DISTRICT

PORT

The district that produces port wine begins about thirty miles inland from Oporto and extends to the Spanish border. The vineyards are planted on terraces that are specially laid out along the steep hillsides of the valley of the river Douro. Port wine is grown and made in a specified district called the Douro, must test at least 18° (Gay-Lussac), and must be shipped from Oporto. As in every wine-growing country, the crop varies every year. Nevertheless, the production of port wine for the past ten years averages almost ten million gallons a year. England imports about half the yearly production. The standard gauge of a pipe of port wine is 115 gallons (522 liters) or 690 bottles.

MADEIRA

Madeira Island, about four hundred miles from the Portuguese coast, produces very excellent but heavy wine, a fairly dry kind and a very sweet one. It is still said that long sea voyages are necessary to greatly improve this famous product.

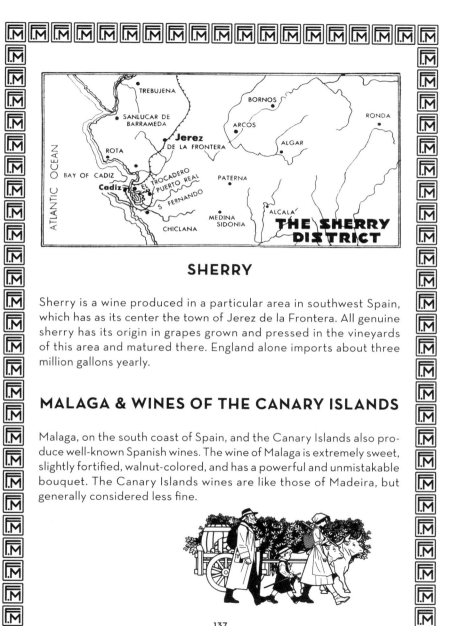

The Sherry District

SHERRY

Sherry is a wine produced in a particular area in southwest Spain, which has as its center the town of Jerez de la Frontera. All genuine sherry has its origin in grapes grown and pressed in the vineyards of this area and matured there. England alone imports about three million gallons yearly.

MALAGA & WINES OF THE CANARY ISLANDS

Malaga, on the south coast of Spain, and the Canary Islands also produce well-known Spanish wines. The wine of Malaga is extremely sweet, slightly fortified, walnut-colored, and has a powerful and unmistakable bouquet. The Canary Islands wines are like those of Madeira, but generally considered less fine.

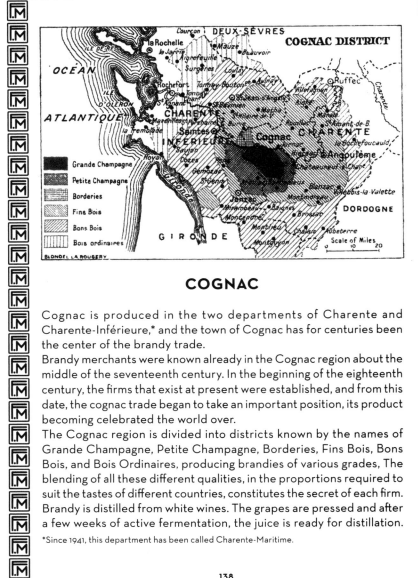

BLONDEL LA ROUGERY

Legend:
- Grande Champagne
- Petite Champagne
- Borderies
- Fins Bois
- Bons Bois
- Bois ordinaires

COGNAC DISTRICT

COGNAC

Cognac is produced in the two departments of Charente and Charente-Inférieure,* and the town of Cognac has for centuries been the center of the brandy trade.

Brandy merchants were known already in the Cognac region about the middle of the seventeenth century. In the beginning of the eighteenth century, the firms that exist at present were established, and from this date, the cognac trade began to take an important position, its product becoming celebrated the world over.

The Cognac region is divided into districts known by the names of Grande Champagne, Petite Champagne, Borderies, Fins Bois, Bons Bois, and Bois Ordinaires, producing brandies of various grades, The blending of all these different qualities, in the proportions required to suit the tastes of different countries, constitutes the secret of each firm. Brandy is distilled from white wines. The grapes are pressed and after a few weeks of active fermentation, the juice is ready for distillation.

*Since 1941, this department has been called Charente-Maritime.

The apparatus used in the Charente is the pot still. The liquid obtained is the delicious brandy called cognac. It is drawn off into good new oak casks, to be stored for years until it has mellowed by age, reduced in strength by evaporation, colored by the wood, and gained the inimitable aroma for which old cognac brandy has become famous.

**"Good brandy is the living soul of good wine.
It has left its body, but it liveth."**

André-Louis Simon

ARMAGNAC

Armagnac comes from the district of the same name in the department of Gers, southeast of Bordeaux. Most of that fine product is made by small land and vineyard owners, and, unlike cognac brandies, is distilled at a considerably lower degree; it is heavier and matures more quickly.

CALVADOS

Calvados, or apple brandy, is made in the department of Calvados in Normandy. Distilled from cider, it is delicious when properly aged.

MARC

Marc is another kind of brandy and is distilled from the residue of pressed grapes. Marc de Bourgogne and Marc de Champagne are the most renowned.

VERMOUTH

Vermouth, *Wermut* in German or wormwood in English, is white wine fermented in the sun, fortified with alcohol and rendered aromatic by adding herbs and spices. The two best vermouths made in France are Noilly-Prat and Chambéry. Italy also produces several high-class vermouths, of which Martini is the best known; they are generally very sweet, being made mostly of muscat grapes.

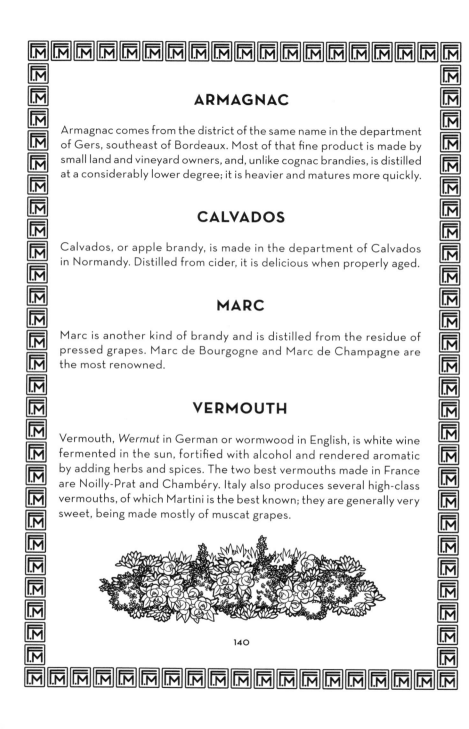

V.
USEFUL
FORMULAS

IN CASE OF POISON INGESTION*

First: send for a physician. Second: induce vomiting by tickling the throat with a feather or a finger; drink hot water, strong mustard, and water; swallow sweet oil or egg whites. Acids are antidotes for alkalis and vice versa.

POISONS & THEIR ANTIDOTES
"Life's cares are a poison and wine, its best antidote."

Acids—muriatic, oxalic, acetic, sulfuric (oil of vitriol), nitric (aqua fortis)	Soap suds, water, magnesia, lime.
Prussic acid	Dash ammonia water in face.
Carbolic acid	Whiskey or dilute grain alcohol, flour, and water, mucilaginous drinks.
Alkalis—potash (potassium hydroxide), salt of hartshorn (ammonium carbonate), lye (sodium hydroxide), ammonia	Vinegar or lemon juice in water.
Arsenic—rat poison, Paris green (copper acetoarsenite)	Milk, raw eggs, sweet oil, lime water, flour, and water.
Lead, saltpeter, corrosive sublimate (mercury chloride), lead sugar (lead acetate), blue vitriol (copper sulfate)	Egg whites or milk in large doses.
Chloroform—chloral, ether	Dash cold water on head and chest. Artificial respiration.
Carbonate of soda, iron sulfate, cobalt	Soap suds and mucilaginous drinks.
Iodine—antimony, antimony and potassium tartrate (tartar emetic)	Starch and water, astringent infusions, strong tea.
Mercury and its salts	Egg whites, milk mucilages.
Opium—morphine, laudanum; paregoric soothing powders or syrup	Strong black coffee, hot bath. Keep awake and moving at any cost.

*Under no circumstances should Frank Meier's recommendations be followed. They are reproduced only for the purpose of preserving the original text. His advice is potentially harmful to the reader's survival!

USEFUL PRESCRIPTIONS

Angostura bitters with soda water, brandy and soda water, the Morning Glory Fizz, and the Morning Glory Daisy are helpful concoctions for a hangover (see recipes).

Bass Ale or any English ale is the least harmful thing to take against sleeplessness.

Champagne will be found as the best remedy for flying sickness and seasickness.

Headache can be cured by sniffing strong pastis. One glass of strong pastis drunk neat and very slowly will also cure neuralgia.

Indigestion can be cured with Fernet-Branca and Italian Vermouth before meals, and after meals with Fernet-Branca and crème de menthe (see recipes).

The best drink to cure a sore throat is a Koldkure (see recipe).

Honey mixed with brandy, whiskey, etc., hot or cold, is also good remedy for colds (see recipes).

The Highbinder (see recipe) will cure diarrhea.

To prevent a cold or influenza, take a Grog or Mulled Wine before retiring to bed (see recipes).

Quinine, aspirin, or Indian Tonic water with a little lemon juice are good remedies for a fever.

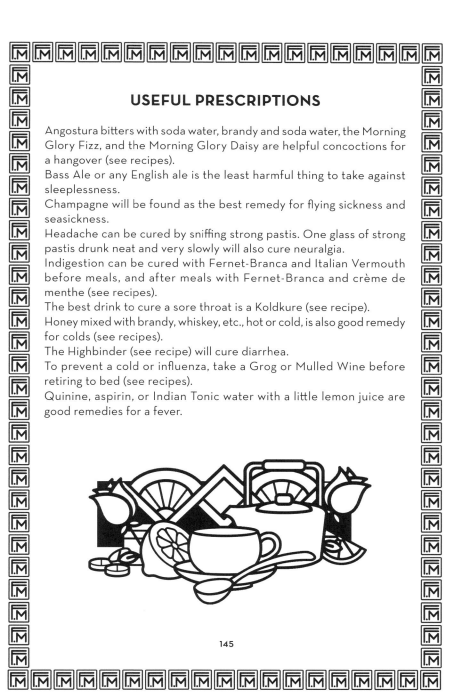

ALCOHOL—COMPARATIVE STRENGTHS*

Gay-Lussac	Sykes	American	Cartier
57.1	Proof	14.2	
57	0.2 u.p.	14	
56	2.0	12	21
55	3.7	10	
54	5.4	8	
53	7.1	6	20
52	8.8	4	
51	10.6	2	
50	12.3	Proof	
49	14.1	2 u.p.	19
48	15.9	4	
47	17.6	6	18
46	19.4	8	
45	21.2	10	
44	23.0	12	
43	24.8	14	
42	26.5	16	17
41	28.3	18	
40	30.0	20	
39	31.8	22	
38	33.6	24	16
37	35.4	26	
36	37.2	28	
35	38.9	30	
34	40.6	32	
33	42.3	34	
32	44.1	36	15
31	45.9	38	
30	47.6	40	
29	49.3	42	
28	51.0	44	

*In Germany and Russia, the Tralles system is in common use. It is the equivalent of the Gay-Lussac system.

TIME DIFFERENCES*
Noon in Paris

Adelaide	9:30 p.m.	Chicago	6:00 a.m.
Mexico City	6:00 a.m.	San Francisco	4:00 a.m.
Amsterdam	12:00 p.m.	Constantinople	3:00 p.m.
Montreal	7:00 a.m.	Santiago, Chili	9:00 a.m.
Athens	2:00 p.m.	Copenhagen	1:00 p.m.
Moscow	3:00 p.m.	Sardinia	1:00 p.m.
Auckland, N.Z.	12:00 a.m.	Cuba	7:00 a.m.
New Orleans	6:00 a.m.	Singapore	8:00 p.m.
Berlin	1:00 p.m.	Gibraltar	12:00 p.m.
New York	7:00 a.m.	Sofia	2:00 p.m.
Bombay	5.30 p.m.	Hobart	11:00 p.m.
Oslo	1:00 p.m.	St. Louis, U.S.A.	6:00 a.m.
Brindisi	12:00 p.m.	Hong Kong	8:00 p.m.
Ottawa	7:00 a.m.	Stockholm	1:00 p.m.
Brisbane	10:00 p.m.	Jerusalem	2:00 p.m.
Panama	7:00 a.m.	Suez	2:00 p.m.
Brussels	12:00 p.m.	Leningrad	3:00 p.m.
Peking	8:00 p.m.	Sydney	11:00 p.m.
Bucharest	2:00 p.m.	Lisbon	12:00 p.m.
Perth (W.A.)	8:00 p.m.	Tokyo	9:00 p.m.
Budapest	1:00 p.m.	Madeira	11:00 a.m.
Philippines	8:00 p.m.	Toronto	7:00 a.m.
Buenos Aires	9:00 a.m.	Madras	5.30 p.m.
Prague	1:00 p.m.	Vancouver	4:00 a.m.
Cairo	2:00 p.m.	Madrid	1:00 p.m.
Quebec	7:00 a.m.	Vienna	1:00 p.m.
Calcutta	5:30 p.m.	Malta	1:00 p.m.
Rangoon	6.30 p.m.	Winnipeg	6:00 a.m.
Cape Town	2:00 p.m.	Mauritius	4:00 p.m.
Rio de Janeiro	9:00 a.m.	Yokohama	9:00 p.m.
Ceylon	5:30 p.m.	Melbourne	11:00 p.m.
Rome	1:00 p.m.		

*Official time differences during Frank Meier's lifetime.

NAUTICAL MILES

The circumference of the Earth is divided into 360 degrees, each degree containing 60 nautical miles. Consequently, the circumference of the Earth, namely 131,385,456 feet divided by 21,600 (360 x 60) gives the length of a nautical mile, which is 6,082.66 feet, and is generally considered the standard.

1 statute mile = 5,280 feet
1 degree = 69.121 statute miles

The nautical mile and geographical mile are now accepted as 6,080 feet. The small difference between the two values is as follows:

	Based on 6,080 ft.	Based on 6,082.66 ft.
1 nautical mile	1.15 statute mile	1.152 statute mile
25 nautical miles	28.78 statute miles	28.8 statute miles
1 statute mile	.8684 nautical mile	.868 nautical mile
25 statute miles	21.71 nautical miles	21.7 naut. miles

1 kilometer = 0.62 statute mile = 1,094 yards = 3,280.8 feet
8 kilometers = approximately 5 miles

The French, German, and Austrian nautical mile is 6,076 feet in length. The knot is a measure of speed, the speed of one knot being a speed of one nautical mile per hour.

To convert statute miles into nautical miles multiply statute miles by 0.8684; to convert nautical miles into statute miles, multiply nautical miles by 1.1515.

THE EARTH

The superficial area of the Earth is 196,950,000 square miles: 139,440,000 square miles of water and 57,510,000 square miles of land. The equatorial circumference of the earth is 24,902 miles; the meridional circumference, 24,860 miles.

The Earth is divided into 360 degrees. The length of one degree of longitude is 69.121 miles. Each degree of longitude represents four minutes of time. The lines of longitude are called meridians.

The diameter Earth is 7,926.677 miles at the equator and 7,899.988 miles through the poles.

The weight of the earth has been estimated at six sextillion, 592 quintillion tons, not including the atmosphere, the weight of which has been estimated at more than five quadrillion short tons.

The average elevation of the land above sea level is approximately 2,800 feet. The average depth of the ocean below sea level is 12,500 feet. The deepest place in the ocean yet found is in the Mindanao Trench, between the Philippines and Japan, where soundings of 34,210 feet have been reported. The highest mountain is Mount Everest, in the Himalayas, at 29,141 feet.

Over two billion people live on the globe and currently speak 2,800 different languages.

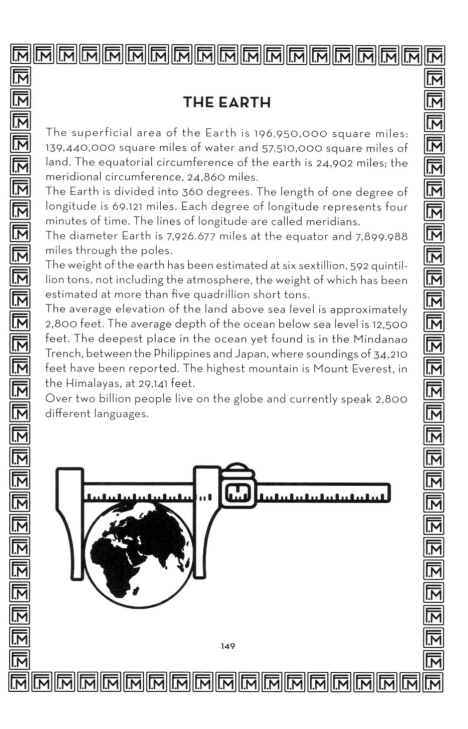

151

PRESSURE

1 kilogram per square centimeter = 14.228 pounds per square inch.
1 pound per square inch = .0703 kilograms per square centimeter.
Steam rising from water at its boiling point (212° F/100° C) has a pressure equal to the atmosphere (14.7 pounds per square inch).

To evaporate one cubic foot of water requires the consumption of 7.5 pounds of ordinary coal, or about one pound of coal to one gallon of water.

One-sixth of tensible strength of plate multiplied by thickness of plate and divided by one-half the diameter of boiler gives safe working pressure for tubular boilers. For marine boilers, add 20 percent for drilled holes.

No plate or bars of either steel or iron should be worked at a black or blue heat (about 500° F/260° C); the material will stand far more strain either red hot or cold, whereas at an intermediate point, great risks will be run and possible strains produced that will later result in rupture.

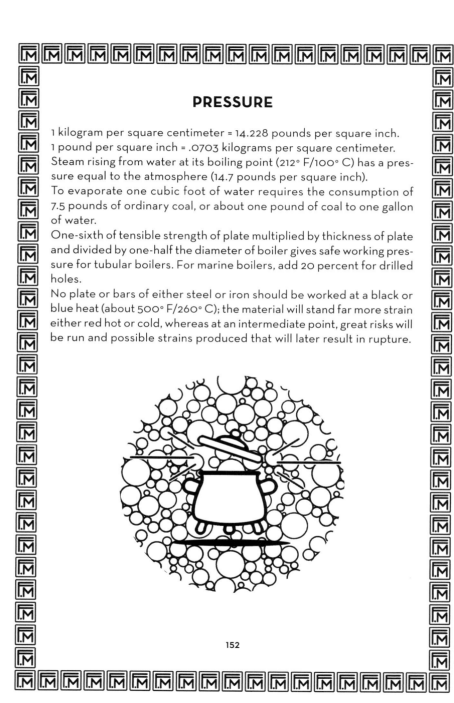

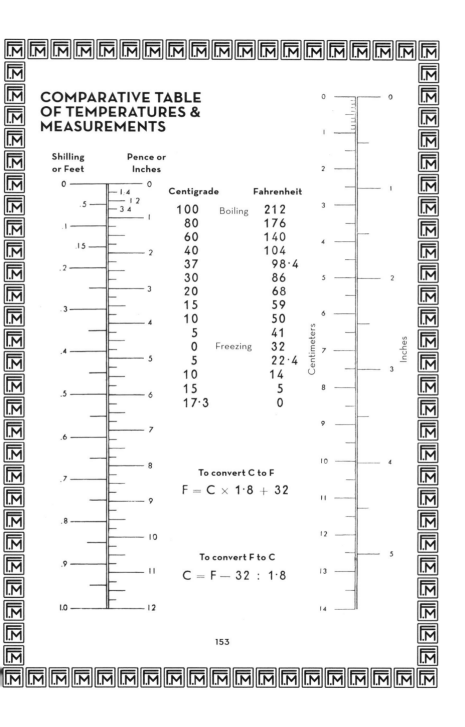

COMPARATIVE TABLE OF TEMPERATURES & MEASUREMENTS

Shilling or Feet

Pence or Inches

Centigrade		Fahrenheit
100	Boiling	212
80		176
60		140
40		104
37		98·4
30		86
20		68
15		59
10		50
5		41
0	Freezing	32
5		22·4
10		14
15		5
17·3		0

To convert C to F

$$F = C \times 1·8 + 32$$

To convert F to C

$$C = F - 32 : 1·8$$

Centimeters

Inches

WEIGHTS & MEASURES

100 kilograms = 267.93 troy pounds or 220.462 pounds

	Cwt	Qtrs	St	Lbs	Oz	Dr	Gr	Equivalents
Tons (U.K.)	20	80	160	2240				1,016,0475 kg
Hundredweights		4	8	112	2240			50.8024 kg
Quarters			2	28				12.7006 kg
Stone				14				6.3503 kg
Pounds					16	256	7000	453.5926 g
Ounces						16	437.5	28.3493 g
Drams							2711	1.7718 g
Troy grains								6.4799 cg

CARATS

The weight of precious stones is given in metric carats; a metric carat is divided into one hundred cent-carats.

One metric carat = 0.2 gram.

For pearls, the grain is used. One grain equals ¼ carat or 0.05 gram and is divided into one hundred parts.

There are weights for the carat, multiples, and submultiples. They are used for precious stones and pearls. Special weights in grains do not exist.

To obtain a weight in grains, multiply the weight in carats by four.

1 gram = 5 carats = (5 x 4) 20 grains.

1 carat = 0.2 gram; 1 grain = 0.05 gram.

The carat is correctly used as expressing the degree of fineness, but not as a weight.

Pure gold is described as twenty-four carats.

If a gold coin (or any other gold object) is, for example, 24, 22, 20, 18, 14, or 9 carats, then it contains 24, 22, 20, 18, 14, or 9 parts of pure gold, and the remaining parts are alloy.

Therefore we may consider that a golden jewel at:

22 carats has a standard of	0.915
20	0.832
18	0.750
14	0.593
9	0.375

But these standards are observed only when an official Law of Control is imposed, as in France.
0.950 is the standard for platinum used in jewelry and works of art.
For silverware, 0.950 – 0.800 are the standards.

CLOTH MEASURE

2 ¼ inches = 1 nail; 4 nails = 1 quarter; 4 quarters = 1 yard

CUBIC MEASURE

1,728 cubic inches = 1 cubic foot
27 cubic feet = 1 cubic yard
128 cubic feet = 1 cord (wood)
40 cubic feet = 1 ton (shipping)
231 cubic inches = 1 U.S. standard gallon
2150.42 cubic inches = 1 standard bushel
1 cubic foot = about four-fifths of a bushel

DRY MEASURE

2 pints = 1 quart   4 pecks = 1 bushel
8 quarts = 1 peck   36 bushels = 1 chaldron

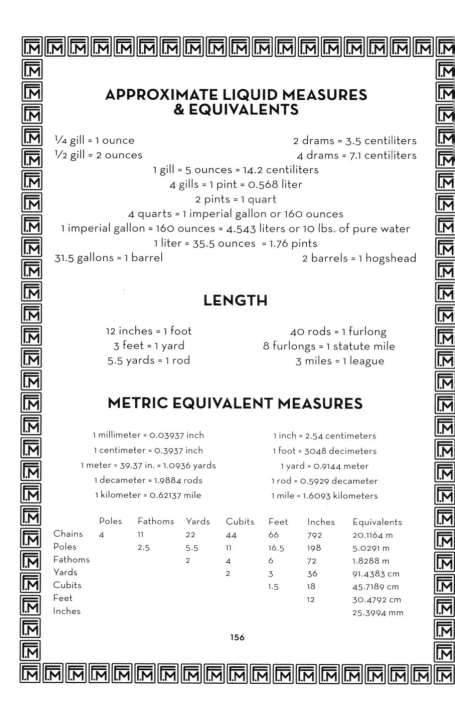

APPROXIMATE LIQUID MEASURES & EQUIVALENTS

¼ gill = 1 ounce

½ gill = 2 ounces

2 drams = 3.5 centiliters

4 drams = 7.1 centiliters

1 gill = 5 ounces = 14.2 centiliters

4 gills = 1 pint = 0.568 liter

2 pints = 1 quart

4 quarts = 1 imperial gallon or 160 ounces

1 imperial gallon = 160 ounces = 4.543 liters or 10 lbs. of pure water

1 liter = 35.5 ounces = 1.76 pints

31.5 gallons = 1 barrel

2 barrels = 1 hogshead

LENGTH

12 inches = 1 foot

3 feet = 1 yard

5.5 yards = 1 rod

40 rods = 1 furlong

8 furlongs = 1 statute mile

3 miles = 1 league

METRIC EQUIVALENT MEASURES

1 millimeter = 0.03937 inch

1 centimeter = 0.3937 inch

1 meter = 39.37 in. = 1.0936 yards

1 decameter = 1.9884 rods

1 kilometer = 0.62137 mile

1 inch = 2.54 centimeters

1 foot = 3048 decimeters

1 yard = 0.9144 meter

1 rod = 0.5929 decameter

1 mile = 1.6093 kilometers

	Poles	Fathoms	Yards	Cubits	Feet	Inches	Equivalents
Chains	4	11	22	44	66	792	20.1164 m
Poles		2.5	5.5	11	16.5	198	5.0291 m
Fathoms			2	4	6	72	1.8288 m
Yards				2	3	36	91.4383 cm
Cubits					1.5	18	45.7189 cm
Feet						12	30.4792 cm
Inches							25.3994 mm

1 square centimeter	=	0.1550 square inch
1 square decimeter	=	0.1076 cubic square feet
1 square meter	=	0.1196 square yards
1 are	=	3.954 square rods
1 hectare	=	2.47 acres
1 square kilometer	=	0.386 square mile
1 square inch	=	6.452 square centimeters
1 square foot	=	9.2903 square decimeters
1 square yard	=	0.8361 square meter
1 square rod	=	0.2529 are
1 acre	=	0.4047 hectare
1 square mile	=	2.59 square kilometers

1 acre = 0.4047 hectare = 40.47 ares = 4.840 sq. yards
= 160 sq. rods = 10 square chains
1 sq. mile = 2.59 sq. kilometers = 259 hectares = 640 acres
or 3,097.600 sq. yards

SQUARE MEASURE

144 sq. inches = 1 square foot
40 sq. rods = 1 rood
9 sq. feet = 1 square yard

4 roods = 1 acre
30¼ square yds = 1 square rod
640 acres = 1 square mile

SURVEYOR'S MEASURE

7.92 inches = 1 link; 25 links = 1 rod; 4 rods = 1 chain
10 sq. chains or 160 sq. rods = 1 acre
640 acres = 1 sq. mile; 36 sq. miles (6 miles sq.) = 1 township

TIME

60 seconds = 1 minute; 60 minutes = 1 hour; 24 hours = 1 day
7 days = 1 week; 28, 29, 30, or 31 days = 1 calendar month
30 days = 1 month in computing interest
365 days = 1 year; 366 days = 1 leap year

TROY POUNDS

	Oz	Dwt	Grains	Mites	Equivalents
Troy pound	12	240	5760	115200	373.2419 g
Troy ounce		20	480	9600	31.1035 g
Pennyweight			24	480	1.5551 g
Troy grains				20	6.4779 cg
Mite					3.2399 mg

The unit of mass for gold and silver is the troy pound of twelve ounces. The ounce is twenty pennyweights of twenty-four grains each. For diamonds, the troy ounce is divided into 151 ½ carats, making six carats equal to about nineteen grains. For pearls, it is divided into 600 grains, making five pearl grains equal to four troy grains.

1 grain = .06479 gram
1 troy ounce = 31.193 grams
1 troy pound = .4536 kilogram
1 gram = 15.432 grains
1 dram = 1.7718 grams

USEFUL FORMULAS

To convert inches to meters, multiply by .0254.
To convert inches to centimeters, multiply by 2.54.
To convert centimeters to inches, multiply by .3937.
To convert kilos to pounds, multiply by 2.2046.
To convert liters to gallons, multiply by .22.
To convert gallons to liters, multiply by 4.548.
To convert grains to grams, multiply by .0648.
To convert ounces to grams, multiply by 28.349.

USEFUL INFORMATION

To find the diameter of a circle, multiply the circumference by .31831.

To find the circumference of a circle, multiply the diameter by 3.1416.

To find the area of a circle, multiply the square of the diameter by .7854.

To find the surface of a ball, multiply the square of the diameter by 3.1416.

To find the cubic inches in a ball, multiply the cube of diameter by .5236.

Doubling the diameter of a pipe increases its capacity by four.

Double riveting is between 16 to 20 percent stronger than single riveting.

One cubic foot of bituminous coal weighs from forty-seven to fifty pounds.

One cubic foot of anthracite coal weighs about fifty-three pounds.

One ton of coal is equivalent to two cords of wood for steam purposes.

There are nine square feet of heating surface to each square foot of grate surface.

The average consumption of coal for steam boilers is twelve pounds per hour for each square foot of grate surface. One horsepower is equivalent to raising 33,000 pounds one foot per minute, or 550 pounds one foot per second. Each nominal horsepower of a boiler requires thirty to thirty-five pounds of water per hour.

To sharpen dull files, lay them in dilute sulfuric acid until they are eaten deep enough.

A gallon of water (U.S. Standard) weighs 8.5 pounds and contains 231 cubic inches.

A cubic foot of water contains 7.5 gallons, 1,728 cubic inches, and weighs 62.5 pounds.

A bottle of wine averages $\frac{1}{6}$ of a gallon or $26\frac{2}{3}$ ounces.

Wallpaper: $11\frac{1}{2}$ yards long, 21 inches wide.

To find the pressure in pounds per square inch of a column of water, multiply the height of column in feet by .434

WIND PRESSURE

Miles per hour to pounds per square foot

Miles per hour	Feet per minute	Feet per second	Force in lbs. per sq. foot	Description
1	88	1.47	.005	Hardly perceptible
2	176	2.93	.02	
3	264	4.40	.044	Just perceptible
4	352	5.87	.079	
5	440	7.33	.123	Gentle breeze
10	880	14.67	.492	
15	1320	22	1.107	Pleasant breeze
20	1760	29.3	1.968	
25	2200	36.6	3.075	Brisk gale
30	2640	44	4.428	
35	3080	51.3	6.027	High wind
40	3520	58.6	7.872	
45	3960	66.0	9.963	Very high wind
50	4400	73.3	12.3	Storm
60	5280	88.0	17.712	
70	6160	102.7	24.107	Strong storm
80	7040	117.3	31.488	
100	8800	146.6	49.2	Hurricane

FOR CLEANING VARIOUS SUBSTANCES

Alabaster: Use strong soap and water.

Black silk: Brush and wipe thoroughly, lay on a table with the side intended to show facing up; sponge with hot coffee strained through muslin; when partly dry, iron.

To remove stains or grease from oil paint: Use bisulfide of carbon, turpentine spirits, or, if the stain is dry and old, chloroform. These and tar spots can be softened with olive oil and lard.

Stains, iron rust, or ink from vellum or parchment: Moisten the spot with a solution of oxalic acid. Absorb quickly with blotting paper or cloth.

Rust from steel: Take half an ounce of emery powder mixed with one ounce of soap and rub well.

Fruit spots on cotton: Apply cold soap, then touch the spot with a paintbrush or feather dipped in chlorate of soda, then immediately dip fabric in cold water.

Grease stains on silk: Take a lump of magnesia, rub it wet on the spot, let it dry, then brush the powder off.

Iron rust: May be removed from white goods with sour milk.

Scorch stains on white linen: Lay in bright sun.

Oil marks on wallpaper: Apply a paste of cold water and pipe clay, leave it on overnight, and brush off in the morning.

Paint spots on clothing: Saturate with equal parts of turpentine and ammonia spirits.

To clean wallpaper: Rub with a flannel cloth dipped in oatmeal.

Black cloth: Mix one part of ammonia spirits with three parts warm water, rub with sponge or dark cloth, clean with water, rub in the direction of the nap of the fabric.

Fingerprints on furniture: Rub with a soft rag and olive oil.

Chromos: Wipe lightly with a damp linen cloth.

Zinc: Rub with a piece of cotton cloth dipped in kerosene, afterward with a dry cloth.

Vegetable stains on hands: Rub with raw potato.

Paint on window glass: Remove with a strong solution of soda.
To clean tinware: Common baking soda applied with moistened newspaper and polished with a dry piece will make it look like new.
To remove dog urine from carpets or rugs: Rub with gin.

HELP IN CASE OF ACCIDENT*

Drowning: 1. Loosen clothing if any. 2. Empty lungs of water by laying body on stomach and lifting it by middle so that the head hangs down. Jerk the body a few times. 3. Pull tongue forward, using handkerchief, or pin with string if necessary. 4. Imitate motion of respiration by alternately compressing and expanding the lower ribs about twenty times a minute. Alternately raising and lowering the arms from the sides up above the head will stimulate the action of the lungs. Let it be done gently but persistently. 5. Apply warmth and friction to extremities. 6. By holding the tongue forward, closing the nostrils and pressing the "Adam's apple" back (so as to close the entrance to the stomach), direct inflation can be tried. Take a deep breath and breathe forcibly into the mouth of the patient, compress the chest to expel the air, and repeat the operation. 7. Do not give up. People have been saved after hours of patient, vigorous effort. 8. When patient begins breathing, get them into a warm bed, give them warm drinks of spirits in teaspoonfuls, along with fresh air and quiet.

Burns and scalds: Cover with baking soda and apply wet cloths. Use egg whites and olive oil (or linseed oil), plain or mixed with chalk or whiting.

Lightning: Dash cold water over the person struck.

Sunstroke: Loosen clothing. Get patient into shade and apply ice cold water to head.

*Frank Meier's recommendations must not be followed without careful consideration and medical knowledge.

Mad dog or snake bite: Tie cord tight above wound. Suck the wound and cauterize with caustic or white-hot iron at once or cut out adjoining parts with a sharp knife.

Venomous insects' stings, etc.: Apply weak ammonia, oil, salt water, or iodine.

Fainting: Place flat on back; allow fresh air and sprinkle with water.

Cinders in the eye: Roll soft paper up like a lamp lighter and wet tip to remove, or use a medicine dropper to draw it out. Then rub the other eye.

Open wounds: On scratches and slight wounds, apply half strength iodine. Dirty or greasy wounds should first be cleansed with high grade benzine. All open wounds should be covered with gauze and bandage from a first-aid kit. Never wash or touch a wound or the part of the gauze that comes in contact with the wound. Never use cobwebs, tobacco, waste, or oil, as they may cause blood poisoning.

HORSE RACING

The ancients had chariot races, the Romans raced riderless horses, but real horse racing had its inception in England, where race meetings were already held, as records show, in Smithfield, in 1174.

Henry VIII arranged for the first racing at Chester; James I built a course at Newmarket in 1607, and during his reign, the three ancestors of all thoroughbreds—Byerley Turk, Darley Arabian, and Godolphin Arabian—were imported from Arabia.

Charles I gave a cup to be raced for in Hyde Park. Charles II instituted autumn races at Newmarket and occasionally rode in races there. The Royal Ascot dates from the time of Queen Anne, the first race being held on August 11, 1711.

The Doncaster St. Leger, so called after Colonel St. Leger, was first run in 1776. Three years later, the 12th Earl of Derby inaugurated the Oaks, named after his seat, "The Oaks."

The following year, the same nobleman founded the world's greatest classic, The Derby, run for the first a time over a mile on May 4, 1780,

worth £1,100; the race was won by Diomed, who was later sent to America. Nowadays, the race is over a mile and a half, is generally run on the first Wednesday in June, and the value has so increased that in 1935 it was worth nearly £10,000 to Bahram, owned by H. H. the Aga Khan.

Four foreign horses have won this classic: the French-bred Gladiateur in 1865, the Hungarian-bred Kisber in 1875, the American horse Iroquois in 1881, and the French-trained Durbar in 1914. Gladiateur also won the Two Thousand Guineas, the St. Leger, and the Ascot Gold Cup; however, he was not the first French horse to win in England—this honor belongs to Jouvence, who in 1853 won the Goodwood Cup. Goodwood races were established in 1802, the Goodwood Cup being given in 1812. The Two and One Thousand Guineas came in 1809 and 1814, respectively; the Manchester Cup in 1816, the Cesarewitch and the Cambridgeshire in 1839. A. K. Macomber, an American owner, won both these autumn handicaps in 1925 with Forseti and Masked Marvel.

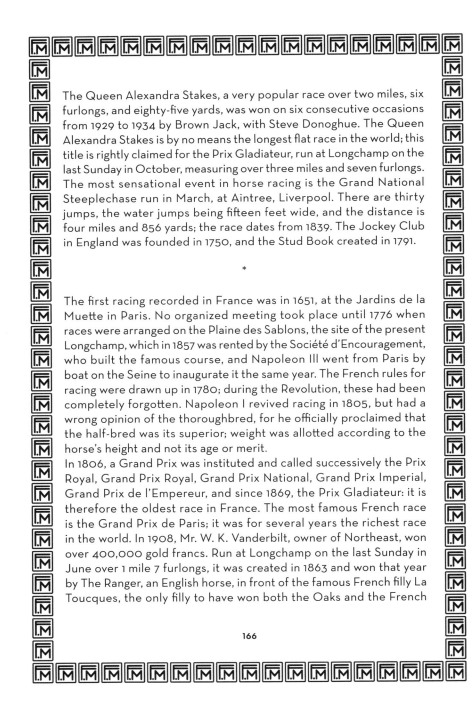

The Queen Alexandra Stakes, a very popular race over two miles, six furlongs, and eighty-five yards, was won on six consecutive occasions from 1929 to 1934 by Brown Jack, with Steve Donoghue. The Queen Alexandra Stakes is by no means the longest flat race in the world; this title is rightly claimed for the Prix Gladiateur, run at Longchamp on the last Sunday in October, measuring over three miles and seven furlongs. The most sensational event in horse racing is the Grand National Steeplechase run in March, at Aintree, Liverpool. There are thirty jumps, the water jumps being fifteen feet wide, and the distance is four miles and 856 yards; the race dates from 1839. The Jockey Club in England was founded in 1750, and the Stud Book created in 1791.

*

The first racing recorded in France was in 1651, at the Jardins de la Muette in Paris. No organized meeting took place until 1776 when races were arranged on the Plaine des Sablons, the site of the present Longchamp, which in 1857 was rented by the Société d'Encouragement, who built the famous course, and Napoleon III went from Paris by boat on the Seine to inaugurate it the same year. The French rules for racing were drawn up in 1780; during the Revolution, these had been completely forgotten. Napoleon I revived racing in 1805, but had a wrong opinion of the thoroughbred, for he officially proclaimed that the half-bred was its superior; weight was allotted according to the horse's height and not its age or merit.

In 1806, a Grand Prix was instituted and called successively the Prix Royal, Grand Prix Royal, Grand Prix National, Grand Prix Imperial, Grand Prix de l'Empereur, and since 1869, the Prix Gladiateur: it is therefore the oldest race in France. The most famous French race is the Grand Prix de Paris; it was for several years the richest race in the world. In 1908, Mr. W. K. Vanderbilt, owner of Northeast, won over 400,000 gold francs. Run at Longchamp on the last Sunday in June over 1 mile 7 furlongs, it was created in 1863 and won that year by The Ranger, an English horse, in front of the famous French filly La Toucques, the only filly to have won both the Oaks and the French

Derby. Fourteen English horses have won the Grand Prix; Galloper Light, Comrade and Lemonora are the winners since the resumption of that race after the Great War.

Edmond Blanc, brother of Camille Blanc, of Monte Carlo fame, who raced very successfully for over forty years, won the Grand Prix on no fewer than seven occasions, and in 1903 his colts Quo Vadis, Caius, and Vinicius filled the first three places, a feat that will stand for many years. In 1899, he paid the colossal sum in those days of one million francs (about £40,000) for the English Derby winner Flying Fox.

The formation of the Société d'Encouragement in November 1833 led to the creation of the Jockey Club, the Stud Book, and later the classical races: the Prix d'Essai des Poulains in 1841, the Prix d'Essai des Pouliches in 1841, the Prix de Diane in 1843, the Prix du Jockey Club in 1836, and the Grand Prix de Paris in 1863. The Prix du Jockey Club or French Derby was first run at Chantilly and was won by a horse named Frank owned by Lord Henry Seymour, the famous dandy, known in history as "Milord l'Arsouille." To the five classic races mentioned above, the Prix de l'Arc de Triomphe was added in 1920.

The Auteuil Steeplechase (Paris), the most beautifully laid out stee-plechase course, has existed since 1873. The best known of the many events run there are the Grand Steeple-Chase (6,500 meters), the Grande Course de Haies, and the Prix des Drags, which are run res-pectively on Sunday, Wednesday, and Friday of the "Grand Week" at the end of June.

*

In America, the importation of a thoroughbred dates back to 1730 and the first races were held in South Carolina in 1734. A genealogical register called the "Stud Book" became an established custom as early as 1829. Horse races are popular in most of the states. The principal events, like the Kentucky Derby and the Oaks are run in Louisville, Kentucky.

The Belmont Stakes, the Futurity, the Withers, the Lawrence Realization, the Swift, the National Stallion, the Champagne, and the

Ladies' Handicap are held at Belmont Park. The American Derby is run in Washington Park (Illinois). The Chesapeake Stakes in Havre de Grace, the Detroit Derby in Detroit, the Classic Stakes in Arlington, the Great American Stakes in Aqueduct (New York); the Latonia Derby in Latonia (Kentucky), the St. Louis Derby in St. Louis, the Preakness and the Walden Stakes in Pimlico (Maryland); the Saratoga Cup, the Saratoga Special, the Alabama, the Hopeful, and the Travers Stakes in Saratoga. The richest race in America is the Santa Anita Handicap in Los Angeles (worth over $108,000 in 1935). All of these races have heavy future books and are outstanding social events.

There are other countries where thoroughbred horses are run before huge crowds of the elite, like Belgium, with the Internationale in Ostend, and Italy with the Derby and the Regina Elena Cup in Rome and more recently the million lire Steeplechase at Merano (Tyrol). Germany has important races at Berlin and Baden-Baden, and both Vienna and Budapest turn out very big crowds for thoroughbred racing, while all Australasia is brought to a fever pitch over the Melbourne Cup.

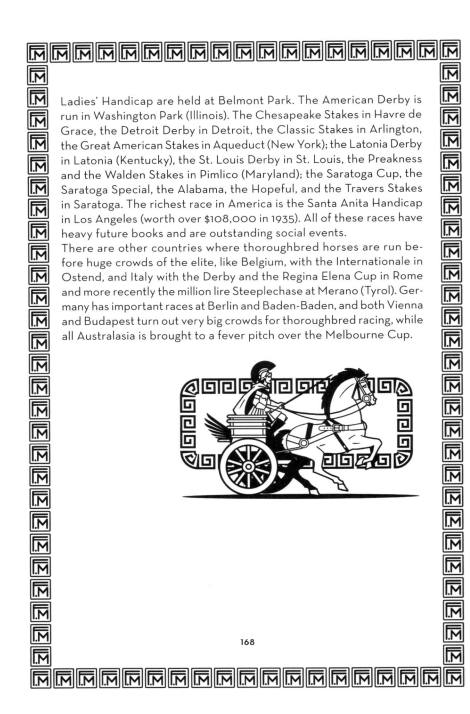

INDEX

ABSINTHE Nº 1 & Nº 2   29
ABSINTHE (FRENCH STYLE)   29
ADONIS   29
AFFINITY   29
ALASKA   29
ALE FLIP   77
ALE, PORTER, OR STOUT SANGAREE   92
ALEXANDRA   30
ALEXANDRA SPECIAL   30
ALFONSO XIII   30
ALMAZA   30
AMERICAN BEAUTY   104
AMERICAN FIZZ   73
AMERICAN GROG   100
AMERICAN ROSE   104
AMERICANO   104
ANGEL'S KISS   30
ANGOSTURA & GINGER ALE   104
ANGOSTURA & SODA   104
ANGOSTURA LEMONADE   82
APPETISER   30
APPLEJACK   30
APPLEJACK (OR CALVADOS), GIN, RUM, OR WHISKEY SOUR   97
APPLEJACK OR CALVADOS TODDY   98
APRICOT OR PEACH BRANDY, GIN, RUM, OR WHISKEY PUNCH   86
APRICOT BRANDY COOLER   63
APRICOT BRANDY, BRANDY, RUM, SLOE GIN, OR WHISKEY RICKEY   89
AUTOMOBILE   30

BACARDI   30
BACARDI FIZZ   73
BACARDI ZOOM   99
BALTIMORE EGG NOG   69
BARBOTAGE OF CHAMPAGNE   105
BARMAN'S DELIGHT   105
BEE'S KISS   31
BEE'S KNEES   31
BÉNÉDICTINE COCKTAIL   60
BENTLEY   31
BETWEEN THE SHEETS   31
BIJOU   31
BISHOP   105
BISMARCK OR BLACK VELVET   105
BISMARCK FIZZ OR SLOE GIN FIZZ   73
BLACK ROSE   105
BLACK STRIPE   105
BLACKTHORN   31
BLOODHOUND   31
BLUE BIRD   31
BLUE BLAZER   100
BOBBY BURNS   32
BOOMERANG   32
BORDEAUX CHAMPAGNE   105
BOSOM CARESSER   106
BOSTON FLIP   77
BRAIN DUSTER   32
BRANDY   32
BRANDY & HONEY   106
BRANDY OR RUM BLAZER   101
BRANDY COBBLER   61
BRANDY, RUM, OR WHISKEY COLLINS   62
BRANDY OR RUM COOLER   63
BRANDY CRUSTA   64

BRANDY DAISY   68
BRANDY FIX   72
BRANDY FIZZ   73
BRANDY OR EGG FLIP   77
BRANDY HIGHBALL   78
BRANDY, CLARET, RUM, OR WHISKEY LEMONADE   82
BRANDY PUFF   84
BRANDY PUNCH   86
BRANDY SANGAREE   92, 101
BRANDY SCAFFA   93
BRANDY SHRUB   94
BRANDY OR RUM SHRUB— COLD   94
BRANDY, GIN, OR WHISKEY SKIN   101, 106
BRANDY SLING   101
BRANDY SMASH   96
BRANDY SOUR   97
BRANDY, GIN, PEACH BRANDY, RUM, OR WHISKEY TODDY   98
BRANDY, GIN, OR WHISKEY ZOOM   99
BROKEN SPUR   32
BRONX   32
BROOKLYN   32
BUBY   32
BUCK'S FIZZ   73
BUNNY HUG   32
BURR   32
B. V. D.   33
BYRRH   33
BYRRH CASSIS   106
CAFÉ & KIRSCH—COLD   106
CAFÉ DE PARIS   33
CANADIAN   33
CARUSO   33
CASSISCO   106

CHABLIS OR POUILLY		DOM.	37	GIN BUCK	107
CUP	65	DOUGLAS	37	GIN, RUM, OR WHISKEY
CHAMBÉRY FRAISE	104	DUBONNET	37	CRUSTA	64
CHAMPAGNE	33	DUBONNET CITRON	107	GIN, RUM, OR WHISKEY
CHAMPAGNE COBBLER	61	DUBONNET FIZZ	74	DAISY	68
CHAMPAGNE JULEP	79	DUNLAP	37	GIN, RUM, OR WHISKEY
CHAMPAGNE PICK-		EAST INDIA	38	FIX	72
ME-UP	33	EDWARD VIII	38	GIN FIZZ	74
CHAMPAGNE PUNCH	86	EGG LEMONADE	82	GIN, RUM, OR WHISKEY
CHATTERLEY	33	EGG NOG	69	FLIP	77
CHINESE	33	EGG NOG—HOT	69	GIN, PEACH BRANDY, RUM,
CHRISTMAS PUNCH	86	ELEGANT	38	OR WHISKEY HIGHBALL	78
CHRISTMAS PUNCH—HOT	86	ELK'S OWN	38	GIN, RUM, OR WHISKEY
CIDER	36	EMERALD	38	PUFF	84
CIDER CUP	65	ENCORE	38	GIN RICKEY	89
CINZANO	36	ESKIMO	107	GIN, PORT, RUM, SHERRY, OR
CLAM JUICE	36	EVANS	38	WHISKEY SANGAREE	92, 101
CLAM JUICE COCKTAIL	112	EYE OPENER	107	GIN SCAFFA	93
CLARET OR BURGUNDY		FASCINATOR	39	GIN, RUM, OR WHISKEY
CUP	65	FAVORITE	39	SLING	95, 101
CLARET OR BURGUNDY		FERNET MINT	39	GIN, RUM, OR WHISKEY
PUNCH Nº 1	87	FERNET VERMOUTH	39	SMASH	96
CLARET OR BURGUNDY		FISH HOUSE PUNCH	87	GIN SPIDER	107
PUNCH Nº 2	87	FOGHORN	107	GINGER ALE CUP	66
CLARET COBBLER	61	FOURTH DEGREE	39	GLOOM CHASER	40
CLOVER CLUB	36	FRANK'S REFRESHER	107	GOLDEN CLIPPER	40
CLOVER LEAF	36	FRANK'S SPECIAL	39	GOLDEN FIZZ	74
COFFEE	36	FRANK'S SPECIAL GIN		GOLDEN FLEECE	107
COLUMBIA SKIN	101	FIZZ	74	GOLDEN SLIPPER	40
CORA	36	FRANK'S SPECIAL PUNCH	85	GRAPE JUICE CUP	112
CORONATION	36	FRENCH VERMOUTH	39	GRAPEFRUIT CUP	66
CORPSE REVIVER Nº 1	36	FRUIT LEMONADE	82	GRAVES	40
CORPSE REVIVER Nº 2	106	FUTURITY	39	GREEN HAT	108
CROCKER	37	F. Y. C. S. (FLORIDA YACHT		GREENBRIAR	40
CURAÇAO PUNCH	87	CLUB SPECIAL)	39	GRENADINE & KIRSCH	108
DAIQUIRI	37	GENEVER	40	GRENADINE GIN FIZZ	74
DEAUVILLE	37	GIBSON	40	GUARDS	41
DERBY	37	GIMLET	40	HAPPY HONEY ANNIE	41
DIAMOND FIZZ	73	GIN	40	HARVARD	41
DIKI-DIKI	37	GIN & IT (GIN & ITALIAN)	40	HAWAIIAN	41
DOCTOR	37	GIN & SIN	40	HAWAIIAN COOLER	63
DOG'S NOSE	106	GIN & TONIC	107	HIGHBINDER	41

HOFFMAN HOUSE	41	MAI WEIN CUP	66	PEACH BRANDY & HONEY,
HOFFMAN HOUSE OR		MAIDEN'S BLUSH	45	RUM, & HONEY, OR
CREAM GIN FIZZ	74	MAJESTIC (OTTO'S		WHISKEY & HONEY	109
HOLLAND GIN FIZZ	74	SPECIAL)	45	PEACH CUP	66
HOMESTEAD	41	MAMY TAYLOR	108	PERFECT	47
HORSE'S NECK	108	MANHATTAN	45	PICK-ME-UP	109
HOT BENEFACTOR	101	MAPLE LEAF	45	PICON-GRENADINE	109
HOT BRANDY	102	MARTINI (DRY)	45	PINEAPPLE FIZZ	75
HOT GIN, RUM, OR		MARTINI (MEDIUM)	45	PINEAPPLE JULEP	79
WHISKEY	102	MARTINI (SWEET)	45	PINK GIN	47
HOT PORT OR SHERRY	102	MARY PICKFORD	45	PINK LADY	47
H. P. W.	41	MILK & SELTZER OR MILK		PIPE LINE	47
H. R. W.	41	& VICHY	113	PISCO PUNCH	87
ICED APRICOT BRANDY	60	MILK PUNCH	87, 102	PLANTER'S	47
ICED CHOCOLATE	112	MILLION DOLLAR	45	PLANTER'S PUNCH	87
ICED COFFEE	113	MILLIONNAIRE	45	PLUNGER	47
ICED TEA	113	MIMOSA OR CHAMPAGNE		POLLY'S SPECIAL	47
IMPERIAL FIZZ	74	ORANGE	108	POMPADOUR	48
INGRAM	41	MINT JULEP	79	PORT	48
IRISH ROSE	108	MONKEY GLAND	46	PORT COBBLER	61
IRISH WHISKEY	44	MORNING BRACER	109	PORT FLIP	78
IRISH WHISKEY COOLER	63	MORNING GLORY DAISY	68	PORT NEGUS	102
IRISH WHISKEY FIZZ	74	MORNING GLORY FIZZ	75	PRAIRIE OYSTER	48
ITALIAN VERMOUTH	44	MORNING SMILE	109	PRESIDENTE	48
JACK ROSE	44	MOSELLE CUP	66	PRINCE OF WALES	109
JOHN OR TOM COLLINS	62	MULLED WINE OR		PRINCETON	48
JUBILEE FIZZ	75	HOT CLARET	102	QUAKER	48
KALTE ENTE	66	N. C. R.	46	QUATRE PAVÉS SPECIAL	48
KING'S PEG OR BRANDY		NEW ORLEANS FIZZ	75	QUEEN'S	48
& CHAMPAGNE	108	NICKY'S FIZZ	75	QUEEN'S PEG OR GIN &
KNICKERBOCKER	44	OLD FASHION	46	CHAMPAGNE	109
KOLDKURE	108	OLYMPIC	46	R. A. C. (ROYAL
LAST ROUND	44	OPAL	46	AUTOMOBILE CLUB)	48
LEAVE IT TO ME	44	ORANGE BLOSSOM	46	RACQUET CLUB	49
LEMON FLIP	77	ORANGE FIZZ	75	RAINBOW	110
LEMON SQUASH	82	ORANGEADE	82	RASPBERRY LEMONADE	83
LEMONADE (PLAIN)	82	ORGEAT FIZZ	113	RAY LONG	49
LEVIATHAN	44	ORGEAT LEMONADE	82	REMSEN COOLER	63
LONDON FOG	44	OYSTER	46	RHINE WINE OR MOSELLE
LONE TREE	44	PARADISE	46	& SELTZER	110
MACKA	108	PARISETTE	113	RHINE WINE COBBLER	61
MAGNOLIA	108	PARISIAN	47	RHINE WINE CUP	67

ROB ROY	49	SHROVE	53
ROBINSON CRUSOE	49	SIDE CAR	53
ROCK & RYE	110	SILVER	53
ROMAN PUNCH	88	SILVER FIZZ	76
ROSE	49	SILVER STREAK	53
ROSEY SQUASH	113	SINGAPORE SLING	95
ROSSI	49	SLOE BERRY	53
ROSSLYN	49	SODA	53
ROYAL	49	SOUR GIN FIZZ	76
ROYAL GIN FIZZ	75	SOUTHERN CROSS	53
ROYAL ROMANCE	49	SOUTHSIDE FIZZ	76
ROYAL SMILE	49	SOYER AU CHAMPAGNE	110
RUBY FIZZ	75	SPARKLING RHINE WINE	
RUM OR WHISKEY		CUP	67
COBBLER (WHISKEY)	62	SPICED RUM	102
RUM FIZZ	76	S. S. MANHATTAN	53
RUM, BRANDY, GIN, OR		S. S. WASHINGTON	54
WHISKEY JULEP	79	STAR	54
RUM SCAFFA	93	STAR DAISY	68
RUM SHRUB	94	STINGER	54
RUSSIAN	52	STONE FENCE	110
SARATOGA	52	STONE WALL	111
SARATOGA COOLER	64	STRAWBERRY FIZZ	76
SAUTERNES COBBLER	62	STRAWBERRY LEMONADE	83
SAUTERNES CUP N°1	67	STRAWBERRY PUNCH	88
SAUTERNES CUP N°2	67	SUISSESSE	54
SAUTERNES PUNCH	88	SUMMER DELIGHT	113
SAZERAC	52	SURE RELIEF	54
SCOTCH WHISKY FIZZ	76	SWEDISH PUNCH—HOT	88
SCOTCH WHISKY		TEMPTATION	54
COOLER	64	TEXAS FIZZ	76
SEAPEA "C. P."	76	THIRD DEGREE	54
SENSATION	52	TIN ROOF	54
SEVENTY-FIVE ("75")	52	T. N. T.	54
SHAMROCK	52	TOM & JERRY	103
SHANDY GAFF	110	TOM MOORE	54
SHANGHAI	52	TOMATE	111
SHERRY	52	TOMATO JUICE	55
SHERRY & EGG	110	TOP SPEED	55
SHERRY COBBLER	62	TRINITY	55
SHERRY FLIP	78	TROPICAL	55
SHERRY NEGUS	102	TUXEDO	55

VALENCIA	55
VELVET CUP	67
VERMOUTH CASSIS	111
VIOLET FIZZ	76
WARD EIGHT	55
WHISKEY	55
WHISKEY SCAFFA	93
WHITE	55
WHITE LADY	56
WHITE PLUSH	111
WHITE ROSE	56
WHITE SHADOW	56
WHIZ-BANG	56
WINTER SPORT	56
YALE	56
YASHMAK	56
ZAZA	56
ZAZARAC	56
ZENITH COOLER	64

First published in the United States
of America in 2025 by
Rizzoli International Publications, Inc.
49 West 27th Street
New York, NY 10001
www.rizzoliusa.com

Originally published in French
in this brand new adaptation in
2024 as *L'Art du cocktail par le
barman légendaire du Ritz* by
Éditions Albin Michel, Paris, France
www.albin-michel.fr
© Éditions Albin Michel, 2024

The publisher disclaims liability for any
outcomes that may occur as a result of any
of the experiences described in this book.

The US edition includes measures
for the cocktail recipes.

For Rizzoli
Publisher: Charles Miers
Editor: Klaus Kirschbaum
Assistant Editor: Emily Ligniti
Managing Editor: Lynn Scrabis
Text Editor: Christiana Hills

ISBN: 978-0-8478-4786-0
Library of Congress Control Number:
2024944933

Printed in China
2025 2026 2027 2028 / 10 9 8 7 6 5 4 3 2 1

Visit us online:
Instagram.com/RizzoliBooks
Facebook.com/RizzoliNewYork
X: @Rizzoli_Books
Youtube.com/user/RizzoliNY

MIX
Paper | Supporting
responsible forestry
FSC
www.fsc.org
FSC® C104723